About Island Press

Since 1984, the nonprofit organization Island Press has been stimulating, shaping, and communicating ideas that are essential for solving environmental problems worldwide. With more than 1,000 titles in print and some 30 new releases each year, we are the nation's leading publisher on environmental issues. We identify innovative thinkers and emerging trends in the environmental field. We work with world-renowned experts and authors to develop cross-disciplinary solutions to environmental challenges.

Island Press designs and executes educational campaigns, in conjunction with our authors, to communicate their critical messages in print, in person, and online using the latest technologies, innovative programs, and the media. Our goal is to reach targeted audiences—scientists, policy makers, environmental advocates, urban planners, the media, and concerned citizens—with information that can be used to create the framework for long-term ecological health and human well-being.

Island Press gratefully acknowledges major support from The Bobolink Foundation, Caldera Foundation, The Curtis and Edith Munson Foundation, The Forrest C. and Frances H. Lattner Foundation, The JPB Foundation, The Kresge Foundation, The Summit Charitable Foundation, Inc., and many other generous organizations and individuals.

The opinions expressed in this book are those of the author(s) and do not necessarily reflect the views of our supporters.

Dream Play Build

Dream Play Build

Hands-On Community Engagement for Enduring Spaces and Places

James Rojas and John Kamp

ISLANDPRESS | Washington | Covelo

Library of Congress Control Number: 2021945118

All Island Press books are printed on environmentally responsible materials.

Manufactured in the United States of America
10 9 8 7 6 5 4 3 2 1

Keywords: art, community engagement, creativity, experiential learning,
inclusiveness, Los Angeles, outreach, play, psychology, urban planning,
South Colton, values, workshop, walkability

To our grandmothers, for encouraging us to dream, play, and build

Contents

Preface

The origins of the ideas in this book are deeply personal—which makes sense, because cities are deeply personal, too. Although the majority of *Dream Play Build* combines our perspectives as true coauthors, we wanted to take a moment in the beginning to share our individual experiences and motivations. We hope our stories inspire you to think about how your interests and experiences might inform your own endeavors to create more-effective modes of community engagement, and, by extension, better cities and places.

James's Story: The Personal Roots of Place It!

Growing up, I wanted a dollhouse, but in those days boys didn't play with dolls. The second-best option, blocks, my family couldn't afford. So instead, my grandmother gave me a shoebox full of recycled objects. Out of the box I created two rooms, and with the objects I created a sofa—out of scraps of aluminum—and a carpet of clear plastic, which I placed the sofa on (see fig. P-1). I still remember not just the finished product but also the process of creation itself: I was able to think about space and shape it, which felt empowering and inspired me to make more.

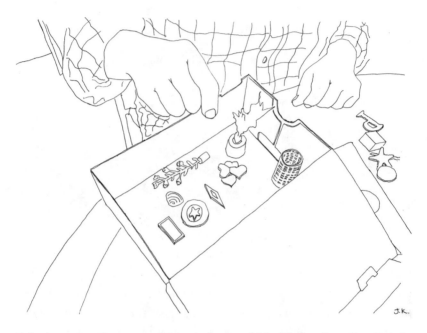

P-1. An imagined version of James's first model-building endeavors, which he explored with a shoebox and simple found objects. (Illustration by John Kamp.)

Around that time, I had become fascinated with looking at Los Angeles through the rear window of my parents' car. I saw hills, mountains, old windmills, cows, and the patterns created by the rows of orange groves. Yet I also started to see change. I saw hilltops disappear, new skyscrapers overtake City Hall, and freeways rip through my neighborhood. Modernism was removing my favorite landmarks. While I felt a sense of real loss, LA's rapid urban transformation became my next muse.

Moving from the confines of the shoebox, I expanded my endeavors out to the bedroom itself and the yard just beyond. For hours

I would lay out streets and buildings on the bedroom floor; out of mud in the yard, I would sculpt and mold hills and imaginary rivers, placing little homemade buildings in and around the landscape. My first attempts to build a city involved just a wash of random objects from my shoebox, all jumbled together. Then I discovered how streets help to organize objects into little neighborhoods. Through these early hands-on activities I started to learn that vacant spaces became buildings, big buildings replaced small ones, and landscapes always changed. And a satisfaction came from transforming my urban experiences and aspirations into these small dioramas.

Most children outgrow playing with toys, but I didn't. Building small cities became my hobby as I continued to find objects to express architecture and landscapes in new ways. I also started capturing the urban experiences from cities I would visit; I became fascinated with San Francisco's hills, and, after a family trip there, I spent months building cities on slopes.

After high school, I studied interior design at Woodbury University. This program helped me express my creativity with new tools, teaching me to understand people's emotional connection to space through color, texture, and form. I was particularly fascinated by how space could be manipulated to create a certain feeling. However, after I graduated I could not find a design job. Not only was the job market weak at the time, but also Latinos were scarce within the profession. Much to everyone's surprise, I decided to join the army, with the promise of being stationed in Europe. In essence, it was a poor man's European vacation.

Rather than quickly visit Europe like a tourist, I had four years to immerse myself there. I was stationed in Heidelberg, Germany, and in Vicenza, Italy. During this time I visited many other cities by train and spent hours exploring them by foot. Woodbury's interior design education had actually prepared me well to examine the effects of geography and urban design on how I felt in various European cities. The natural light, weather, and landscape varied from city to city, as well as how residents used space—from

Heidelberg's pink sandstone buildings to Florence's warm-colored buildings. I was also fascinated by how European streets and plazas had been laid out like outdoor rooms with focal points and other creature comforts. I felt very much at home within the Italian piazzas in particular, as they recalled the boisterous public life I had known in East Los Angeles.

The backdrop to my entire experience in Europe was the liberation of not having to drive. As such, I could feel the different public spaces through my senses. It was in this way that I realized public spaces could be experienced in intimate sensory ways— much the same way that Americans experience the private spaces of their homes.

When I ultimately chose to come back to the United States, I knew a complete 180 awaited me: I'd once again be driving everywhere. Perhaps as a coping mechanism, I told myself to embrace driving like I had done with walking in Europe. However, what sounded like a convincing idea from afar proved difficult to execute once back home. Stuck in LA's traffic, my body craved the sensory-rich experiences I had had in Europe. Never being able to recreate what I had felt and experienced there, I decided to attend the Massachusetts Institute of Technology (MIT) to study urban planning and try to understand what I was not just experiencing but also feeling.

At MIT, I struggled to learn technical planning language, so I turned back to the model-building of my pre-Europe years to help me stay focused and relaxed and also make sense of what I was learning. I turned my Room 10-485 studio space into a three-year city-building marathon in which I spent many hours experimenting with new ways of visualizing the urban theories we were learning about in class. Needless to say, my city-model-building techniques became more sophisticated as an indirect result of this formal education in urban planning policy, theory, and history. Meanwhile, I found it peculiar that more of my classmates weren't interested in the sensory experiences or physical aspects of city form; they focused mostly on policy.

Within our learning about policy and history and design was what seemed a hard-and-fast rule of what constituted "good" and "bad" city form. I wondered where the urban design of my Latino barrio of East LA fit in. The community was not as tidy as most American middle-class neighborhoods, yet I had a strong emotional attachment to it all the same. To make sense of this kind of cognitive dissonance, and with a newfound sensitivity to how my surroundings affected my senses, I revisited and roamed the streets of East LA for one year, taking pictures of life on the street and the informal interventions people made to their homes and yards.

Through my wanderings and explorations, I began to realize that what separated Latino LA from the rest of LA was how people used space. Latinos were transforming the hostile auto-centric streets of Los Angeles into intimate, sensory-rich urban places similar to those of Europe. They were using their imaginations, bodies, everyday materials, and land to enhance the social cohesion of the neighborhood. For example, every front yard had a fence around it. While at first glance this seems to be an effort to feel safer, I found that for many residents the fences indicated a longing for the plazas of Latin America. Enclosed by low, wrought-iron, permeable fences, these front yards became an extension of the home. The resulting spaces were often designed and maintained by women. Filled with plants and seating, Victorian lamp posts and fountains, they were inviting spaces that offered a respite from the endless asphalt of the Los Angeles landscape. Exploring them led to a body of research on a new way of looking at and understanding communities that was based not on numbers but rather on memory, needs, and aspirations—the intangibles that shape physical form and lend a sense of place and belonging.

Once I had graduated, I moved back to LA and got a job as a city planner with the City of Santa Monica. I still vividly remember driving home back to my apartment off of Melrose one day and seeing black plumes of smoke covering LA as far as the eye could see. The chaos of LA's 1992 civil unrest had quickly begun unfolding in the streets, rocking my formal planning world. For me, the civil unrest represented a disenfranchised, working-class population and the disconnection between them and the city's urban planners. Why weren't their voices being heard?

My return to LA was troubling and left me longing to be far away. Around that time, the Cold War was officially ending, which presented an unexpected opportunity for me to explore civil society and the built environment through the Peace Corps. I was sent to Budapest and was suddenly no longer behind a desk as a planner but out on the Hungarian streets building environmental awareness. There I found the experiences and opportunities for new knowledge that I had been missing in LA. Where I had once been immersed in freeways, wide streets, and parking structures, I was now steeped in a city exhausted by years of Communist rule but rich with the history embedded in its façades.

In Budapest, the prewar public transit system, rail infrastructure, and land-use patterns were still intact and being used. Riding these historic systems became an everyday experience that stirred my imagination. On transit I watched the *babushkas* holding their worldly possessions in large nylon plaid bags, tourists struggling to read Hungarian, and riders clutching loaves of bread. Then I would just stare out of the window and see architectural details of old wedding-cake buildings along the not-so-blue Danube.

Of course, my romantic notions of Budapest's streetcars and trams were being shattered by the realities of an emerging capitalist economy. The politics, policies, and land uses that had kept public transportation and rail infrastructure intact were crumbling as rapidly as the Berlin Wall. Cars had been kept off the streets of Budapest for almost fifty years; however, after the fall of communism, the city quickly became the dumping ground for used Mercedes and Audis from more well-to-do parts of Europe. The city was completely unprepared to deal with the onslaught of cars, which literally littered the city.

However, bigger forces were at play to dismantle Budapest and

Hungary's rail and transportation system. Western Europe and the budding European Union viewed Eastern Europe, now Central Europe, as the center of trade with Russia. This meant more cars, trucks, and highway-building through Hungary, the Czech Republic, Slovakia, and Poland, and on into Russia.

After three years of living and working in Budapest, I had a completely new understanding of the role of public transportation in shaping cities for the better. My experiences, the environmental campaigns I worked on, and newfound knowledge made me question my old transportation ways in Los Angeles. With my time in the Peace Corps and Hungary coming to a close and a move back to the US and LA imminent, I asked myself, *How can I communicate my transit epiphany to LA drivers who have not had my experiences in Eastern Europe?*

Returning to LA with my newfound knowledge, I worked at the Los Angeles Metropolitan Authority (LA Metro), planning rail lines and bike paths and funding urban design projects. In my free time, I organized professional Latino urban planners to help low-income Latino communities. Community outreach was critical to all these endeavors; however, there were no specific tools with which to engage Latinos in these issues.

By serendipity, I found the solution on Latino LA's streets. While I was working for LA Metro, plans were in the works for a $900-million rail project through East Los Angeles, a core community of Latino Los Angeles. When we held an Eastside transportation meeting to solicit input on the project, about seventy-five low-income Latino residents showed up but offered no comments about the project. At the time, Latino residents had the lowest rates of auto ownership and highest rates of transit use in LA County. From my research, I knew they had more on-the-ground knowledge of using public transit than most of the transportation planners. That's when I realized that our community meetings did not engage Latinos.

While working at LA Metro, a friend, Adrian Rivas, and I opened up the G727 art gallery in downtown LA. Collaborating and learning from artists, I explored the intersection of art and urban planning, and in the process, art became my new muse. I was fascinated by how artists used their imaginations, emotions, and bodies to capture the sensual and sensory experience of landscapes. Through this creative approach, we were able to engage large audiences in participating and thinking about place in different ways, all the while uncovering new urban narratives. While the artists saw their work as expression and representation, I started to see their work as a possible way of reframing urban planning and how urban planning and art could be complementary endeavors. From planners, artists could learn new approaches to understanding the land and cities; from artists, planners could learn new techniques for community engagement.

For artists, the building blocks of a city comprised not only structures, streets, and sidewalks, but also personal experience, collective memory, and narratives. These elements are the less tangible but no less integral elements of a city that transform mere infrastructure into *place*. In this way, artists begin their inquiry by using their imaginations and senses to explore place: *How does the site feel? What do I see or not see? What does the land say?* These are the questions I started wanting to explore through my work by blurring the lines between urban planning and art.

Shortly after we opened the gallery, a new wing of art practice called Social Practice began to emerge in LA. This participatory kind of art focused on engagement through human interaction and collaboration. It valued the art-making process over the finished product or object. And it was the perfect movement for exploring creative city planning, because cities are never a finished product.

I started revisiting my childhood city models and seeing new potential in them: they could be tools for community engagement by giving the public artistic license to imagine, investigate, construct, and reflect on their communities. I began displaying my city models in the gallery and became a kind of merging of urban planner and social-practice artist.

The models both fascinated people and brought them together to imagine and actively design better communities. Through the installations, I directly involved and engaged participants in a creative and collaborative process of city building. The resulting artwork then reflected how varied groups of players—strangers, neighbors, friends—interact to create a sense of place in cities.

Eventually the buzz around the models caught the attention of Doreen Nelson, then a professor at Art Center and Cal Poly Pomona and who is the creator of design-based learning (DBL), a methodology based on John Dewey's learn-by-doing pedagogy. She visited the gallery to see my model and encouraged me to take her DBL course at Art Center. Nelson's aim, no matter who the participant, is for people to come up with completely new ideas for solving problems as opposed to learning how to replicate existing solutions. "The goal is to put the learner in an almost-pretend position," said Nelson in an interview with *Architect* magazine, "as if they're the first people on the planet and they think, 'It's raining outside. I have to get dry.' In that case, I use the word *shelter* instead of *housing*, because if you ask students to design a house, you know what you're going to get."[1] In our course, she taught us how to maximize creativity and engagement in the classroom by asking open-ended questions and using nonrepresentational objects. For her first activity, she had us create our ideal classroom using just Post-it notes. We presented our classrooms to the group and then worked in teams on a design exercise that built off the first one.

While I was the only urban planner in the five-day summer course (everyone else was an educator), I immediately saw the approach's relevance to my own work. *Why not use this approach in city planning?* I thought. Cities are made up of individuals who have to compromise through space. At the end of the day, we plan infrastructure. What better way to communicate this to the public by having them prototype infrastructure and spaces through objects?

So I returned to my childhood shoebox and thought of the objects I had used. Like the tools we had used in Nelson's classes, these objects were nonrepresentational (e.g., a popsicle stick could be part of a bridge or a building and didn't have to just be a popsicle stick). As such, the objects' colors, textures, shapes, and placement could help people capture their feelings and experiences of space rather than keep them confined to just talking about urban space as infrastructure. Through the objects, people could reflect on and articulate their memories, needs, and aspirations. And coupled with prompts such as "Build Your Ideal City," the objects could provide the public with a free form of urban inquiry and expression that went beyond the limitations of the physical form.

Eventually my idea and the ensuing tinkering led to a first proper "project," so to speak. Sojin Kim, a longtime friend who now works at the Smithsonian Institution, asked me if I could help a nonprofit, Taking the Reins, do a participatory workshop to help at-risk Latina youth design a stable to take care of horses. The executive director of the nonprofit insisted on giving the girls miniature horses for their models, yet fresh out of Nelson's course, I knew the pitfalls of being so literal with this kind of creative exercise. So we ended up striking a compromise: we gave half the girls horses and the other half just found objects akin to the ones I had used in my shoebox model as a kid. In the end, the girls who had worked with only found objects produced creative and imaginative stable designs, while the girls with horses ended up dressing them up like dolls and never ended up designing actual stables.

This was 2007 and was really the first Place It! workshop (though the name "Place It!" came later). The workshop generated learning lessons that have shaped our work ever since—in particular, the importance of not placing a premium on perfect scale and using objects that could represent a plethora of things rather than objects that each represent just one thing. A green pipe-cleaner could be a branch of a tree, but it could equally be the edge of a greenspace; whereas a little horse figurine could be, well, a horse and not much more.

From there, we also began pulling from John's background in both the trainings we conducted and urban and landscape design to expand and evolve the workshop format. Initially we didn't ask participants to do any sort of reflection on what they had built, seen, or observed. Yet in order to help participants close the learning loop and continue reflecting on their model-building experiences long after the workshops, we modified the format to include more group-led synthesis and analysis of information throughout the workshop. This synthesis and analysis is now part and parcel of the Place It! method.

To take the work further, capture even larger swaths of constituencies, and generate new layers of information and nuance, we then developed two more methods: the pop-up model, and the site-exploration exercise using our senses, both of which are explored in greater depth in chapter 2. We also began transforming portions of workshop, pop-up, and site-exploration outcomes into more tangible products, such as actual street designs and sections, landscape guidelines, and tree palettes for neighborhoods, among others. Yes, models of imperfect scale that consist of found objects can indeed be translated into to-scale designs for landscapes, streets, and other spaces. However, as we make clear throughout the book and in particular in chapter 7, planners and design professionals have a habit of fixating on the need for tangible outcomes in community engagement and overlooking the value of intangible outcomes in community engagement—fostering group cohesion, learning how to navigate the planning process, learning that we all have creativity and design capacity within us, establishing common values, to name just a few—and thus we are always seeking to expand people's conceptions of what constitutes an "outcome" and move beyond measuring the validity of an engagement method according to whether it resulted in a park, a building, or a plan.

Whatever the outcomes or project objectives, we've seen time and time again that what we now call the *Place It! methods* (i.e., model-building workshop, pop-up model, site exploration using

our senses) effectively push back on and offer up sound alternatives to conventional ways of doing community engagement. They
level the playing field by not favoring one kind of participant over
another. Instead of being focused on language, they are rooted in
participants using their hands and senses to engage in their surroundings, thus leading to creativity and aspiration as opposed
to reaction and replication. And they can be used in a range of
sequences and permutations tailored to match both the objectives
and timeline of a given project: one-off; plan update; large infrastructure project; yearlong planning project—any and all are possibilities and have been done with demonstrated results (which we
discuss in depth in chapter 7).

But consider my story, how Place It! began, how it has evolved,
and what we've observed and learned along the way as not merely a
primer but an invitation—an invitation to not only read further and
learn and discover more but also build off of what we have done
and come up with your own ways of doing community engagement
tailored to the world you live in, ways that both level the playing
field and generate useful results that allow us to dream, to play,
and ultimately to build the kinds of enduring places and spaces in
which we all would like to reside and spend time.

John's Story: A Planner's Search for New Tools

From 2005 to 2008, I worked as a city planner and urban designer
for the City of Los Angeles. When I scan through memories of
my post-community-meeting drives home during those years, the
recurring theme is a feeling of acute hopelessness. In one instance,
I was driving down the I-10 freeway back from Venice after making a presentation, in the gym of a community center, on a new
design overlay for one of the ugliest streets in the United States,
Lincoln Boulevard. We had put together a thoughtful presentation
on, among other topics, urban design principles regarding street-
width-to-building-height ratios that make for a more satisfying

pedestrian experience; on zoning and how it affects building uses and heights; and on the concept of mixed-use buildings (retail on the ground floor, housing up top). The objective of these presentations was always the same: educate the public in core planning concepts so that they could move beyond thinking about traffic and lack of parking and too much density. Upon this planned-for awakening, the residents would then offer up thoughtful ideas regarding building heights and street widths, zoning, mixed use, and other core planning concepts of our age. A perfectly sensible approach, we thought.

I distinctly remember how, after the presentation and during the Q-and-A session on that particular evening, a woman jumped the comment queue, stormed the podium, and proceeded to yell, "I've got something to say! I've got something to say!" What then unfolded was a tirade about having to walk past a trailer park on her way to Whole Foods with her kids and how that just wasn't right and that something needed to be done about that. Other comments, while less vociferous, centered on less traffic, more parking, and keeping building heights low and without any new housing.

On another evening, for another design overlay, we gave a presentation to local residents about what a community design overlay is and then broke out into stations where residents could come up and ask us more specific questions. I was stationed behind a table labeled "Site Planning." A local resident who described herself as an artist parked herself in front of the table and pointed to an area on a map of downtown San Pedro and said confidently, "I'm going to be building a huge sculpture here—as big as the Statue of Liberty. It's going to be like the Statue of Liberty, except"—and here her eyes got wide—"*sexier*." She paused for dramatic effect and continued: "Yes, *sexier*. Because this is *Los Angeles*. It's going to be a *man*"—another pause—"wearing"—pause, wide eyes—"*tight jeans* . . . with maybe a cape, and a guitar with lasers shooting out of it."

Midway through her description of her planned project, I started to hear people singing and turned to my left to see that a gaggle of medieval re-enactors, who had surreptitiously entered the meeting hall during our presentation, had gathered in a dimly lit corner on the opposite end of the room from the break-out stations, and begun singing medieval tunes *a cappella*. I was noticeably distracted, at which point the sculpture artist aggressively quipped, "What, do you have a problem with them singing?" Needless to say, not a lot about site planning was discussed that evening.

In yet another instance, we had put together a presentation on principles of urban design and walkability in the hopes of helping residents in a more well-to-do neighborhood see that a very large proposed development could improve walkability in the neighborhood. After the presentation, we wanted to have residents draw the kind of development they wanted to see, including street sections and rough site plans. While we had hoped that the residents would see the error of their previous ways and want zero-lot-line buildings without lawns because they made for a better pedestrian realm, the residents generally chose not to draw anything and instead just tell us what they wanted: single-family homes, set well back from the street, with large lawns in front.

What springs forth when I look back upon these particular vignettes now is a slightly wide-eyed incredulousness—not just that these things actually happened (they did), but also that we as planners truly thought that a presentation on urban design fundamentals would equip everyday residents with the tools and perspectives to somehow experience a creative and cultural awakening in which constructive feedback on walkable streets and pedestrian-oriented development would flow forth. *But we had put together such a good presentation*, I would think on my drives home while searching for what we could have done to prompt different feedback. I never thought that maybe what we were asking of residents was completely and wildly unrealistic. I also never thought to question whether expecting particular results from those residents was wise or fair.

By the time I had officially chosen to leave the confines of life as a city planner, I saw public participation as just something we did because we had to although it was a waste of time and always generated the same feedback: we want less traffic, more parking, single-story buildings, and no more housing. What I know now is that most forms of community engagement do generate exactly this kind of feedback. Absent a way of taking people out of what they perceive as everyday needs for living, they will invariably default to what they know and experience every day—more traffic, changing neighborhoods, and scarce parking—and then they will want what they perceive as immediate solutions to these problems.

The first glimmers of a solution to this state of affairs emerged in 2007, when James and I did our first model-building workshop together at his art gallery in downtown Los Angeles. We invited anyone and everyone who was interested, with the promise that they could re-imagine Los Angeles by building it. The event was completely unrelated to any plan or proposed project that the City was heading up and was instead simply billed as a kind of merging of crafting, art-making, and community visioning.

The physical set-up was nothing fancy and very un-curated by today's social media standards. Participants gathered around simple folding tables with a colorful construction-paper placemat in front of each chair, and we provided a mountain of found objects off to one side. I set up my turntables and speakers toward the back of the room and then spun house and techno while participants built small models out of found objects that represented their "ideal Los Angeles." (The exercise of building a favorite childhood memory, now a key part of our workshops today, was one that we added later when we started to see a pattern: planners built textbook ideal cities as opposed to cities from the heart; they needed to be shaken out of that mindset of transit-oriented development, nodes and hubs, accessory dwelling units, and all the other prototypi-cal examples of contemporary planning practice and education.) James served as the MC, introducing people to the ideas behind the workshop exercises and then leading them through "report-back" sessions on what they had built. While the specific details of what the participants built are now definitely fuzzy, I do remember the atmosphere well. It was brimming with good cheer and creative energy. People laughed, danced, shared and built off-the-wall ideas, and generally just let themselves unfurl. It was completely unlike what I had experienced on a day-to-day level as a city planner at City-led community meetings.

In deference to accuracy, I will say that the process initially struck me as mere play and perhaps collective art-making, and little more. I was still steeped in the world of professional planning and the notion that a planning education in good design and scale afforded a level of skill and opinion that everyday folks just didn't have—and thus ideas born out of this kind of hands-on event couldn't be useful to planning our cities. Over time, however, my opinion has changed radically. James and I have gradually folded this method into our everyday planning and design work because it has seemed to make sense and, well, is infinitely more fun than a typical community meeting. Along the way, we have continually seen how this process not only taps into people's core creativity and intuitive planning knowledge but also diffuses the anger, frustration, and polarized attitudes that people so often bring to planning meetings.

Engaging people through their hands, senses, and emotions unlocks ideas and expansive ways of thinking that transcend what people know and experience every day. We've seen countless times now that this allows them to imagine new worlds and build ways of getting there (see fig. P-2). The need to somehow engineer outcomes in the way that we used to do (i.e., a presentation on urban design so that participants could then suddenly think differently about streets and sidewalks) is removed, as the medium automatically and tacitly facilitates these ways of thinking differently about our surroundings, oftentimes in ways unforeseen by those of us leading the engagement events. And the entire process allows participants to sink into a state of play in which feelings of antagonism and polarization slip away.

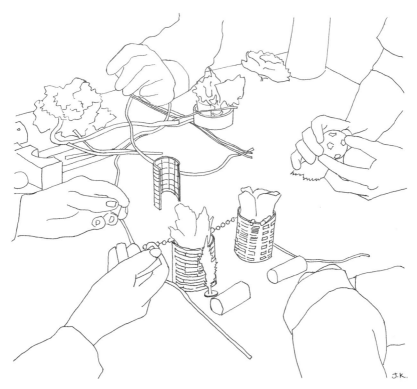

P-2. A sketch of the kind of creative collaboration that unfolds when people work with found objects to build ideal spaces and places. (Illustration by John Kamp.)

Within the stuffy setting of a community meeting on a design overlay, the artist's idea of a Los Angeles version of the Statue of Liberty, with its laser-shooting guitar and tight rocker jeans, seemed surreally comical and underscored everything that was wrong with community engagement at the time. Yet within the context of a Place It!–style workshop, these ideas would feel neither outlandish nor out of place. In fact, they'd probably make everyone say, "I love that. What else can we come up with to make our cities better?"

"*More* lasers!"

"Tighter jeans!"

And on the playful collaboration would go.

To many, it may sound unrealistic and implausible that such a simple process can achieve so much in so little time, but it does. We've seen these results emerge time and time again, with all age groups, ethnic groups, with people in cosmopolitan cities and people living in rural areas, and everything in between. As our work has expanded and evolved, we have developed additional hands-on and sensory-based methods of engagement to create new experiences for participants, unlock additional ways of exploring our urban and natural worlds, and capture new layers of information. We have gone from doing this work as more of an art practice toward something that can empower participants and build relationships while simultaneously leading to the kinds of plans, drawings, designs, spaces, and places that we typically think of as proper "outcomes" (more on that and expanding our conception of "outcomes" in chapter 7).

Ultimately, this book is meant as a guide to lead you toward understanding, with confidence, that what seems like "just play" can lay the groundwork for better outcomes and better lives. If you are professionally involved in the remarkable work of shaping our cities, I invite you to envision how you might make use of some of these methods in your everyday work. But we are all invested in not just the places where we live but also the places where people we know and love live, so this book is also meant to spark ideas for engagement in less formal planning and design—say, a neighborhood gathering in which residents get together and build models of a better neighborhood equipped to tackle the growing host of problems that we as a nation and world are facing.

Even if only 5 percent of the ideas that emerge from the model-building exercises become part of the real world, you will invariably feel as though you know your neighbors better and have an infinitely stronger bond, seeing commonalities where once you might have seen only differences.

As for the other 95 percent of the ideas, it's their creation and their suggestion of possibility that can lift us up and keep us going.

Chapter 1

Forget What You Know about Engagement

Wʜᴀᴛ ᴅᴏ ʏᴏᴜ ᴡᴀɴᴛ ᴛᴏ sᴇᴇ in your neighborhood? What do you want to see in your park? What do you want to see on your street? These are questions that, on the surface, seem inclusive, democratic, and generous. And they are some of the most common ways that towns, cities, and consulting firms—and even community groups—conduct public engagement: hold a visioning session; listen to what people want to see in their neighborhood; record what is said; and weave the feedback into a community plan, an overlay, or some variation thereof. We've done our due diligence, listened to the community; now it is public record, and the neighborhood can change and improve in ways that truly reflect the wishes of its residents.

Tapping into local, on-the-ground neighborhood knowledge is at the core of effective and forward-thinking urban planning and design, landscape design, architecture, and the efforts of everyday residents to better their neighborhoods and communities, as you uncover insights that no outsider, however astute, could on their own; yet merely asking people what they want to see does not

1

always generate the kinds of meaningful feedback that can paint a nuanced and layered picture of the community or of the neighborhood's knowledge and aspirations. In fact, when we are asked point-blank what we want, we oftentimes default to something that contains very little in the way of aspiration or nuance, and instead we focus on perceived threats or immediate needs—the most common being more parking, less traffic, and no density.

Laying a Foundation

The problems of community engagement and the limited outcomes it tends to generate are all too familiar to anyone who has been on either the planning or the public side of the process. Planners get annoyed by the near pitch-perfect predictability of the public's responses (i.e., "More parking! Less traffic! No density!"), while citizens frequently feel as though they are simply not being heard and that whatever input they managed to give never revealed itself in the final plan, development, park, design overlay. While it is tempting to write off community engagement as therefore hopeless, we know from our own work in engaging people with their hands and senses that community engagement can indeed lead to truly creative ideas and a constructively empowered public.

Much of the shift in making community engagement actually worthwhile starts with a solid understanding of the psychology behind modes of engagement and how the medium of engagement directly influences the relative creativity, usefulness, and visionary nature of the outcomes. There are psychological reasons why the most well-thought-out presentation and well-crafted questions will most likely fail to generate useful and creative feedback. There are also psychological reasons why simply shifting ideas from a survey over to Post-it notes on a wall, or packaging them into something crisp and bright for social media, will also likely fail to deliver on creative outcomes and a public who sees their ideas meaningfully reflected in the final planning project at hand.

With this in mind, we invite you to set aside what you know about engagement and public participation and come back to square one, in the same way that we did some years ago when we both clearly knew that what we were doing in our respective planning arenas with community engagement wasn't working. First, we'll lay a foundation of the psychology of survival and creativity, and how creativity really cannot flourish if the participants' concerns, whether they acknowledge them consciously or not, center on simply surviving. Then we'll explore how and why modes of engagement whose primary medium is language—both written and spoken—can hamper expansive ways of thinking. And we'll look at what needs to be in place to fuel people's imaginations within the setting of community meetings and other forums of engagement.

Change Is Coming in the Form of a Cake. What Kind of Frosting Do You Want?

Rarely is community engagement conducted independently of a proposed project or plan. More often than not, by the time a consulting team or crew of planning staff arrives on a neighborhood's doorstep to solicit input, there is already a project in the pipeline. To many residents, this can feel like soliciting feedback on the decoration for a cake that has already been baked—a cake people may not have wanted in the first place. As a result, this approach, however articulately presented and well packaged by consultants or planning staff, can come across as patronizing and disingenuous.

To planning staff, as well as design and consulting teams, the public's negative reaction can be surprising and frustrating—even annoying. Many assume that community engagement in whatever form is a service that is fundamentally good and fundamentally productive: "We're asking you what you think. So what's the problem?"

However, Rebecca Karp, CEO and founding principal of Karp Strategies, who uses model-building and other creative media in her everyday community-engagement work, offers up a perspective that can shed light on why residents can be so angered by the pre-baked-cake approach. "Engagement is largely an activity that is taking from people," said Karp. "You are asking them for their time to tell you what's gone wrong"—or what they do or don't like about a project. Thus, if the very medium of the engagement itself suggests that a project or plan is really going to go ahead with or without their input, people can feel like they've taken time out of their busy lives for nothing, or, worse, that they are powerless in the face of change.

This feeling of powerlessness and frustration is particularly acute for long-disadvantaged communities like the ones Alli Celebron-Brown works with. President and CEO of the McColl Center for Art + Innovation in Charlotte, North Carolina, Celebron-Brown is at the front lines of a neighborhood experiencing rapid change in a city that consistently ranks at the bottom among US cities for potential upward mobility of its residents. "You never want people to share and not be heard," she says. However, when there have been years of not just unsound planning decisions but also redlining, and "essentially doing away with neighborhoods because there were people of color living there," being heard is just the tip of the iceberg. There can be extremely low public trust vis-à-vis the planning process, and the pre-baked-cake approach can only compound that lack of trust.

In an attempt to assuage neighborhood concerns, many planners and designers try to help residents see a bigger picture and understand the City's motivations. To these ends, community engagement meetings on a specific impending planning or building project are frequently prefaced by an educational presentation about a technical aspect of planning or design: zoning, floor-area ratios (FAR), height limits, zero-lot-line buildings, and other fundamentals of urban design and creating inviting public spaces. The reasoning is that if planners and design professionals can broaden the minds—and, by extension, the responses—of participants, they can get public buy-in on the project. For example, if people better understand how street-width-to-building-height ratios affect the walkability of a neighborhood, they will understand that the upcoming project, while tall, would improve everyone's quality of life.

While well intentioned and well thought out, these presentations assume that the limited and predictable outcomes of the community engagement, and the continuing lack of public trust, are a result of a lack of information. However, if the community engagement is conducted in a way that merely solicits feedback on a project that is already going to happen regardless of input, residents will invariably feel patronized and likely be unreceptive to the broader, more philosophical discussion of how the project will contribute to the strengthening of the urban fabric as a whole.

Community Engagement as a Form of Both Exclusion and Competition

Whether it be in the style of an open-format, visioning-style meeting, or soliciting feedback on a particular project or plan, oftentimes only those with the time to spare will show up at a public meeting in the first place. In this way, what appears as a democratic process can, by its very nature, be acutely self-selecting and exclusive.

"The people [in San Francisco] who are accessing opportunities to engage are generally already very privileged," says Robin Abad Ocubillo, senior planner with the City of San Francisco, "and that generally correlates to an older demographic that has the time: people who might no longer have to worry about children or young children, and people who have free evenings, or even the ability to come to a hearing during the middle of the day." Abad Ocubillo's observations also perfectly square with those of Miroo Desai, senior planner for the City of Emeryville, California: "In my experience," she explains, those who attend public meetings "are older—almost all retired." And, she added, they tend to be predominantly White.

A landmark study on the demographics of those who attend and speak at public meetings revealed that public-meeting-goers "are more likely to be older, male, longtime residents, voters in local elections, and homeowners." Further, these attendees are oftentimes present precisely to oppose development. Perhaps unsurprisingly, then, Desai notes that residents rarely attend public meetings to oppose or challenge new office space or, in the case of Emeryville, one of the numerous biotech hubs and centers that have been built or created there. Rather, they show up to challenge new housing and mixed-use retail/residential projects.

Complicating matters further is what takes place once the meetings begin: not everyone will speak. It's a phenomenon that, upon first glance, can not only be puzzling—as in the case of James's account of running community meetings in East Los Angeles on a multimillion-dollar rail-line extension and attendees saying nothing—but also misleading: we predictably but wrongly conclude that those who had opinions spoke, while those who remained silent or didn't show up had no opinions at all.

However, it takes a particular kind of person who is ready and willing to speak in front of a crowd and before a panel, board, or committee. "I'm terrified of public speaking" is a commonplace sentiment. In fact, Patricia Munoz, a licensed family therapist in Los Angeles who uses art and tactile-based activities as a way to engage her clients, notes that of the biggest fears her clients and patients have, public speaking is number one. "Most of us are not born with those skills or are naturally born public speakers," says Muñoz. "It takes a lot of courage and a lot of practice to be good at it. So most people don't do it, even if they want to." And yet, embedded within the statement "I'm terrified of public speaking" is something deeper: a perceived cultural expectation that everyone *should* be good at and comfortable with public speaking. The truth of the matter is that some people will probably never be comfortable with or adept at public speaking. Variations in both learning and communication styles abound among us: some people are more visual learners and communicators; some prefer speaking their minds within a smaller group or even a one-on-one setting. Some express themselves through art; some express themselves through physical activity, including team sports, or even watching sports. The fact remains that *expression* is a relative term and phenomenon that takes many forms, depending on the individual. And that individual's cultural background, where they have grown up, their economic status, among other factors, can play a significant role in shaping their comfort level vis-à-vis different modes of expression.

When it comes to expression within the public meeting setting in particular, an extra layer of complexity exists: the presence or perceived presence of conflict and disagreement. In an era when cities are growing and changing at rapid rates, residents can have particularly strong concerns over and opinions about what their urban future should look like. Invariably, these concerns and opinions can translate into heated debates, disagreements, and sometimes even acute anger. This dynamic can end up excluding all but the most emboldened and those unafraid of conflict. Openly disagreeing with a neighbor and the possibility of retribution from that neighbor can be deal-breakers for many, and thus these individuals will choose to simply remain quiet. So, what appears on the surface as a fair and democratic process—the public meeting where people are free to speak their minds—can inadvertently end up being an exercise in competition, might, and, by extension, exclusion.

Rethinking Talking

Precisely in response to the limitations and drawbacks of conventional community engagement, there have been numerous efforts in recent years to rethink public outreach across the country. We have seen the rise of the Post-it note in public meetings and on boards as a way of both visually recording and prioritizing residents' ideas; we've seen the rise of stickers as a way of giving everyday residents a means of ranking proposed planning ideas. We've also seen a rise in virtual forms of participation: online surveys, apps, and start-ups that seek to be one-stop shops for facilitating a range of information-gathering and measuring results. These companies offer services that cities and municipalities can contract out in order to conduct their engagement and outreach if their planning staff is too busy with other work.

While these attempts to create more meaningful and effective modes of community engagement are welcome alternatives, they fall short on one key point: they still rely heavily on the word, both written and spoken. While language indeed offers up rich opportunities for expression—in essays, literature, poetry, for example—when it serves as the primary medium of expression within community engagement, it tends to be a limiting factor in terms of both who speaks and what is said.

Psychologists who weave art therapy into their practices understand this phenomenon well: what emerges from talking versus using one's hands is oftentimes quite different. Says Munoz of working with some of her younger patients in her family therapy practice, "You will ask them, 'How's school going?' And they'll say, 'Oh fine, oh good.' And I'll ask, 'Is anything going on?' 'No, nothing's going on.'" But then, Munoz will have the young people use objects to play out a scene from their day, or draw a picture, and it becomes clear through the placement of the objects, the story accompanying them, or the scenes depicted within the drawings, that everything isn't just fine, and a lot *has* happened that day, some of which can be quite negative.

Munoz notes an important distinction we are often not aware of: what we are *thinking* versus what we are *feeling*. While we experience these two modes of being simultaneously, what we are thinking can frequently not square up with what we are feeling. And the medium we use to express ourselves can play a key role in which experience—thinking or feeling—is brought to the fore. When we use talking alone to express ourselves, we are using a very particular part of our brains, one that is not known for its creativity. "The talking brain is, loosely speaking, the prefrontal cortex," says San Francisco–based psychotherapist Roché Wadehra, who also uses

art making and non-talk-based modes of expression in her practice. "It's the decision making, the higher functions, the executive
functions [that] they are all focused on there, and developmentally,
that's also the part that starts coming online much later on as we
develop verbal skills." While the prefrontal cortex is there to protect
us, regulating us out of flights of fancy that could, quite bluntly,
lead to harm or death, that very regulatory force is also the one
that can sway us away from creativity, imagination, and an expansiveness in our thinking. This is especially so as we transition into
our late twenties, at which point the prefrontal cortex has generally
fully formed; the executive office of the brain and its predilections
for survival begin to take center stage, and the creative mind so
characteristic of children and young people oftentimes fades into
the background.

As Muñoz points out, what we are doing when we are using
our talking brain is in part focusing on perceived immediate needs
and survival. And if your trip to the community meeting—or your
day in general—involves sitting in traffic, looking for parking, and
dealing with crowds, your talking mind will translate those experiences into both threats and basic needs for survival. "And unless
those things are tackled and taken care of, most of us cannot be creative and cannot think outside the box, because most of us are just
thinking about survival," said Munoz. And so, despite the expertly
crafted presentation by city planners on walkable streets, we will
continue to fixate on something as humdrum as parking, or rightly
focus on past wrongs we feel the city has committed. Wadehra
also adds that in times of great change, this kind of frozen-state
fixation on perceived needs for survival is even more amplified.
"There's just so much change happening so fast that it's a lot for
people to deal with," she says of our current age. Fight, flight, or
freeze/collapse are our natural responses to that extreme change.
For those who have traveled more, lived abroad, and experienced
other cultures, the significant demographic changes the country
has experienced in the past thirty years may seem less of a threat;

for those who have not, it can feel as though threats are all around them. "Someone who has never been out of a particular radius their entire life—it's really hard for them to encounter that kind of globalization," said Wadehra. This sense of being assaulted or in the line of threats from all sides can then hamper any efforts to encourage residents to be more creative in their thinking about their neighborhoods and cities.

Stepping Out of Survival Mode

Getting all of us to a place where we can emerge from survival mode and start to entertain more creative ideas starts, at its core, with creating a space of comfort and ease so that we are open to giving the talking brain a break. "You have to feel safe enough—not completely safe, but safe enough—to be able to play and to get to that state of exploration and curiosity and connection," says Wadehra. In the context of the community meeting or forum, creating this sense of safety can be difficult if the sole focus is on planning and development projects (and, by extension, possible neighborhood change) in the pipeline. Compounding this difficulty is the common insistence on adhering to a strict meeting format that is typically some variation on this theme: introduce staff, introduce project, solicit feedback, end meeting. This format simply does not allow for creating the physical and figurative space in which to be at ease and then be creative.

Fostering the sense of safety necessary for play requires a kind of padding on both ends of the experience, an entry-and-exit ritual— something that is quite common within more overtly play-oriented activities. Sports events, for example, are punctuated by a set of opening and closing rituals. While we take them for granted as simply part of the game experience, the rituals serve to really create a space outside of everyday reality in which play is possible and encouraged. For precisely these reasons, when you're trying to weave play into a community or neighborhood meeting setting, it is imperative to modify the meeting format so that cutting to the chase is not the driving force; instead, a looser entry into the project and activities is. Folks trickle in, unwind, have some food, chat with neighbors, and simply get comfortable. This slow unwinding effectively serves as that entry ritual, allowing us to let our guards down and become open to using our hands, playing, and building.

From there, we can more easily move into a state of play, in which we give the regulatory parts of our brains a rest and fire up not just our creative but our visionary selves. Through play and using our hands, we can tap into new ideas, become aspirational, and engage in expansive ways of thinking that would not be possible if we were still stuck in survival mode. We're also able to shake off the habits and grooves we all invariably get stuck in as we become older. The combined effect of this play and the loosening of old grooves is to experience feelings of excitement, euphoria, and possibility. In our Place It! work, we push boundaries a little by suggesting that folks think of it as a wholesome drug trip, where the outcomes can be more visionary and creative ideas for a neighborhood, and participants can gain a newfound sense of well-being and a connection to their core values. In fact, participants of Place It! workshops frequently describe feelings of elation and a kind of mental expansiveness by the end. "I feel like I'm tingling with ideas and possibilities," one workshop participant said after going through the model-building activities.

Indeed, both Wadehra's and Munoz's expertise and observations in their own fields square perfectly with what we have observed firsthand time and time again when language is the central medium of communication at public meetings: either no one talks, or the same cast of characters talk, and what they say is all too often reactive, occasionally combative, and very rarely imaginative or aspirational. Even when people are given the opportunity to write down what they want to see, the ideas tend to remain anchored to what people know in their everyday world and not shaped by what they dream of or aspire to.

For example, in a recent workshop on climate change that we were a part of but did not lead, participants were simply asked to divide up into groups and write down a list of ideas for how to tackle climate change. Across the board, the responses focused on mere amplifications of what people already knew: more electric vehicles and electric vehicle charging stations. The responses were a pitch-perfect example of those old grooves and habits we get stuck in, here in the form of the everyday car but with the exhaust taken out. However, when we recently built a pop-up model of downtown Los Angeles (see fig. 1-1) at a sustainable engineering conference and had people use their hands to build their ideas for a more climate-resilient, sustainable, and walkable downtown, people built well outside of their current realities and infused the city with their dreams: bioswales, pedestrian zones, unearthing creeks long covered over by asphalt, storage sheds and bathing facilities for homeless people, more light rail, lower curbs, urban farms, more intimately scaled buildings. And the list goes on. In fact, not one person built a model of an electric vehicle or charging station.

Wrap-up and Where We're Headed

The long and short of it is that the community engagement conducted in this country typically generates a false sense that we are really taking the public's pulse on the range of ideas and aspirations found within neighborhoods and communities. In favoring the word and language as the primary medium of expression, and packaging that opportunity for expression within the setting of the public meeting, planners and design professionals generate a particularly limited and skewed set of ideas and opinions, ones that are oftentimes neither rooted in aspiration nor representative of the community as a whole. These approaches also further exacerbate the pervasive problem of low public trust and faith in our governments and civic institutions by failing to involve everyone at earlier stages within the planning and design process and instead asking

1-1. John talking to a conference-goer about her ideas for a greener downtown Los Angeles via the pop-up model we built for a sustainable-engineering conference there.

people to merely comment on what is, at that point, already a historical fact set in motion.

Both Wadehra's and Munoz's observations corroborate what had been little more than hunches to us fifteen years ago, when we were in the early days of developing Place It! as a new mode of community engagement. We had seen the limitations of language-based engagement over and over again and knew we needed to figure out how we could get anyone and everyone dreaming—and dreaming big—about their neighborhoods and communities, and to do so without having to rely on speaking alone to articulate these ideas. We also immediately began seeing the stark contrast in both group dynamics and outcomes between conventional forms of engagement and the hands-on, sensory-based ones we were creating and leading.

These hands-on, sensory-based tools are what we turn to next. We will lead you through a nuts-and-bolts how-to of the core methods that comprise the Place It! approach: the model-building workshop, the pop-up, and the sensory-based site exploration. The idea is to provide you with all the details and tips you need to fold these methods into your own work as well as explorations of your neighborhood and creative efforts to preserve, add to, or create the kinds of enduring spaces and places we all need in our lives.

Chapter 2

Learning to Plan through Play

IN OUR TECH-SOAKED WORLD OF metrics and data, we have a tendency to equate complexity and technical knowledge with value. We also tend to equate simplicity and playfulness with things that have little value beyond what they might offer to kids or our leisure time. And yet when we're trying to engage everyone in the shape and shaping of cities, neighborhoods, landscape, and even transportation systems, playfulness and simplicity are what we need most.

In fact, the core of the Place It! approach is rooted in both simplicity and play. Its very simplicity means that the engagement methods can be easily understood and replicated: anyone can participate, and anyone can learn how to use the methods in their own work and in their own neighborhoods. Its very playfulness means that the methods not only activate parts of our brains that allow for creativity and collaboration but also make the activities, well, fun. In this way, we can maximize both the numbers of those who can participate and also the inventiveness, creativity, nuance, usefulness, and layered nature of the ideas they generate.

In this way, too, we can maximize the number of those who are able to learn the Place It! methods and fold them into their own work and their space- and place-shaping efforts. Thus, this chapter starts from the get-go with the confidence and knowledge that anyone reading this can learn the Place It! approach and weave it into their everyday work of engaging everyone in bettering their surroundings. We go into the nuts-and-bolts of how and when to use these methods and for what objectives, the materials needed for each method, sample breakdowns of the time to spend on each method, and ways of recording the feedback and ideas generated. By the end, you should have the knowledge and confidence to organize and lead your own model-building workshop, build a pop-up model, or conduct a site exploration in which participants use their senses to explore the space. You might also be inspired to come up with your own engagement techniques that are similarly rooted in both simplicity and play, wonder and discovery, exploration and collaboration.

Place It! Method Type 1: Model-Building Workshops

"Model building" can indeed evoke images of precisely cut foam-core or wood glued together to perfection to create small-scale but to-scale versions of existing places or imagined ones. However, our version of "model building" means something very different and much more free-form: we have people build both memories and ideal spaces and places with nothing but found objects—pipe cleaners, Christmas ornaments, buttons, bottle caps, fake leaves—objects anyone, regardless of professional or educational background or learning style, can engage with to make their ideas come to life. And we have them do so in a very short amount of time: 10 minutes, tops. As such, ideas flow quickly and, in a flash, take shape as models. No perfection, no competition, only creativity in its purest form (see fig. 2-1).

We have led model-building workshops all over the country

(and the world, actually), and while they may vary in participant makeup and core goals, they always accomplish something similar: transforming what may start off as a group of strangers into a group of people who see their commonalities, who play and collaborate to literally build the kinds of spaces and places they would like to reside and spend time in.

2-1. *Participants of a Place It! model-building workshop collaborate to build an ideal walking city.*

Why This Kind of Workshop, at What Point, and with Whom?

For both longer-term and midrange planning and design projects, the model-building workshop serves as an effective kick-off-style engagement event to really set a visioning process in motion. It can also be held multiple times in multiple areas to capture different constituencies and audiences. For shorter-term projects or merely one-off events, the model-building workshop can be used as a training method, a means of galvanizing a group or community around an issue, a tool for team-building and bonding for staff, or even a simple classroom exercise. Whatever the case, think of the model-building workshop as a foundation for the establishment of both core values and collective visions.

Indeed, establishing core values across what seem to be differing communities and constituencies can seem challenging; however, the tactile and accessible nature of the activity means that you can easily bring to the fore what all people hold near and dear to themselves. We have led these workshops with everyone from people experiencing homelessness to civic and business leaders, immigrant communities, people of color, urban planners, architects, the LGBTQ community, older Caucasian residents, students of all ages, even law-enforcement officers. And frequently, the workshops contain a mix of folks from several of the aforementioned groups and demographics. Whatever the makeup of the group, the workshops effectively serve to break the ice, create a sense of understanding among participants regardless of differing backgrounds, validate people's lived experiences, and generate real ideas for how to move forward with the issue at hand. In essence, over the course of the workshop, participants find and develop their own roles within the shaping of the world around them.

Venue, Set-up, and Materials

This type of workshop format is ideal for instances in which a constituent group is able to gather at a set location (e.g., a banquet hall, conference room, or community room) for at least an hour and a half, factoring in an additional 15 minutes at the beginning and end for set-up, meet-and-greet, and clean-up.

For larger groups (i.e., more than ten or twelve), the room should be arranged so that participants can gather around smaller tables that seat up to six people comfortably, as the participants will ultimately need to work in smaller teams for the second half of the workshop (see fig. 2-2). For smaller groups, you can have everyone gather around one large table. At least one separate table for model-building materials should be provided for larger groups, while for smaller groups the model-building materials can simply be placed in the middle of the single table. As a practical consideration, be sure to check in advance whether tables will be provided or whether you as the organizer will have to bring them.

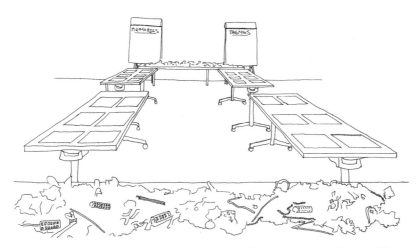

2-2. A sample room arrangement for a model-building workshop, with piles of found objects to the front and back, tables to the center and sides for building models, and two easels easily visible to everyone for recording memories, ideas, and themes. (Illustration by John Kamp.)

As mentioned above, when it comes to supplies, conventional model-building materials such as foamcore, glue, rulers, and X-Acto knives are not required. Rather, you should use the simplest of materials. First, you will need letter-sized colored construction paper. One sheet should be placed in front of every chair at each table prior to participants arriving. These sheets will serve as the bases for each participant's model and for the larger models created in the second half of the workshop. Next, provide as many found objects as you can gather together atop a table in one central location that everyone can access. These objects might include but aren't limited to hair rollers, popsicle sticks, fake leaves, trinkets, figurines, and pipe cleaners. In fact, it is better to use objects that are not immediately recognizable as typical elements of a physical place (i.e., buildings, streets, sidewalks, cars) and instead use objects that could be used to represent a variety of elements within a built and emotional landscape (see fig. 2-3). For example, hair rollers could represent buildings, but they could equally represent a memory of spending time with one's grandmother while she styled her hair. In essence, the choice of objects should allow for maximum flexibility of interpretation and creativity.

2-3. Participants begin mining a pile of found objects for building their models of their favorite childhood memory, which they will build on simple pieces of construction paper.

THE MODEL-BUILDING EXERCISE 1: BUILD YOUR FAVORITE CHILDHOOD MEMORY

The first activity will consist of having everyone build a memory with found objects in 10 minutes. For workshops that are part of a more general, visioning-based planning project, we typically have participants build their favorite childhood memory. However, the prompt can easily be modified to more closely align with the topic of the project at hand. For example, if the workshop is part of a community engagement project for transportation infrastructure improvements, then the prompt could be along the lines of "Build your first memory of a mobility experience" (a prompt we have actually used quite often).

Whatever the case, after 10 minutes of building time are up, every participant will have one minute to describe to the group what their memory is and what they have built.[1] For groups that are not too large, we often like to have everyone stand up and gather around each model as it is presented, so that everyone can get an up-close look at the memory. So as to keep the exercise uplifting and validating, we usually follow every mini-presentation with "Let's hear it for ——" and a summary of the model, and then everyone typically claps. While this perhaps sounds silly, it is one more way of creating the kind of comfortable atmosphere necessary for collective play.

Why Build a Memory?

A common question from both clients and participants unfamiliar with the Place It! method is "Why? Why are we building our favorite childhood memory if we are here to talk about our neighborhoods, communities, and cities?" It is a valid question that deserves a response, both to the clients before the workshop and to participants before everyone gets started with building. At the core, when we mine our best memories from childhood, we are tapping into memories of times when we first felt we belonged, places where we felt safe, into moments of joy and freedom and comfort. The effect of reflecting on that memory and then building it serves to remind ourselves of what our core values are. We not only reaffirm these values to ourselves through the exercise—and even *reconnect* with these values, which oftentimes get lost in the shuffle of the day-to-day realities of just surviving in the world—but in the process of reporting back to the group on what we have built, we also learn about what others value and, more often than not, how similar we all are.

In particularly polarized times and with particularly conflict-laden planning projects, this establishment of similarity and shared experience among participants is of the utmost importance. In one workshop we held in coastal Oregon, we had recent Latino immigrants and older White residents, some of whom were very conservative, all seated around the same tables. They built and shared their favorite childhood memories together and then worked in teams to build their ideal neighborhoods. No conflicts ensued; instead, we saw collaboration.

This collaboration comes about, in large part, when some level of trust and a sense of safety among all participants is achieved. And this safety comes from some sense of familiarity with others—in this case, by way of building and sharing childhood memories and seeing that so often the recurring themes within the memories are shared by many of the other participants—or, to put it in layman's terms: we're not so different after all. The building and sharing of a memory is what Roché Wadehra, the San Francisco–based psychotherapist referenced in chapter 1, refers to as finding "that little soft spot—remembering your childhood. That's the time when we play, when we have permission to play as children." Reflecting on this "soft spot" and this time of play and then seeing that we have all had similar experiences allow us to let our guards down just enough to sink into a state of play and collaborate together. It's an approach that we have found so effective that we keep asking ourselves why the starting point for more conversations and projects at all scales and levels of governance is not such an activity. In the blink of an eye, the sharing of a favorite memory diffuses perceived polarization and conflict (for more on the role of this method in mediation, see chapter 4), and, even better, creates a sense of camaraderie.

Of course, people are oftentimes doubtful that setting the stage for collaboration can happen so quickly and relatively easily. In a recent workshop proposal to a group of academics, we had laid out the flow based on times and the objectives for each activity, allotting our normal amount of time, 15–20 minutes, for a short model-building and sharing exercise on childhood memories. In between that agenda item and the next, we had written, "Now that collective values have been established, we can play and build in teams." A professor wrote back and said, "Establishing collective values in 20 minutes??? Sorry, but this is not possible." And yet we've seen time and time again that it is indeed possible; that the simple act of building childhood memories and sharing them really does set the stage in a very short amount of time for strangers to come together and collaborate.

Because of frequent skepticism around the effectiveness of play, we recommend taking a little time to explain the fundamentals of this approach before beginning the exercise and during conversations with potential clients who will be hosting the workshop. "Whoever you are working with, whoever you are doing engagement for, you need to have an enlightened client who understands that outreach is messy and complex and understands that the value and quality of feedback is only as good as whoever shows up," says Rebecca Karp, who has woven this workshop method into the outreach her firm has done for the redesign of libraries in Brooklyn and on visioning exercises for the Atlanta BeltLine. She has also sometimes seen the need to stray from the strict workshop time of an hour and a half. "If you ask folks to build their first childhood memory, give them however long it's going to take for them to do that. Even before that, let them settle in and eat their snacks."

The extra time at the beginning serves as the kind of entry ritual that, as Wadehra has described, is necessary for setting up a space for play, and the childhood-memory activity allows participants to feel comfortable and valued—integral parts of the process. As a result, they will provide much more nuanced and candid feedback throughout the engagement process and be willing, even eager, to collaborate and be expansive in their thinking.

Reporting Back, Recording Results, and Drawing Out Themes

Once participants have built their memories and are ready to report back, have one person from the team leading the workshop record the participants' memories and what they've built on a flip chart or white board that everyone can see. A seemingly simple but important detail is to write the participant's name first, then the memory and what they built. (It will be impossible to write down the memory word for word, so just use a shorthand that covers the highlights.) The inclusion of a name helps personalize the overall process and further allows participants to feel like their voices matter. Once everyone has reported back, ask participants to look at the responses all together and reflect on what the common themes are. This might take some time, so it is important not to force or rush this portion of the exercise. Write down these common themes in a separate column next to the notes on the memories and models or on a separate flipchart or white board (see fig. 2-4). You will come back to these themes later in the workshop, so leave them up where folks can see them.

The effect of having the participants draw out recurring themes is twofold: first, participants will start to move beyond seeing each model and memory as stand-alone and unrelated to others; and second, participants will more often than not realize how much commonality there is among everyone there—regardless of where a participant is from, their educational background, or their profession.

The Model-Building Exercise 2: Work in Teams to Build an Ideal City, System, Place

After going through everyone's models and the recurring themes together, the workshop dynamic will most likely have shifted ever so slightly. Participants will feel a bit more relaxed, a bit more comfortable, and, ideally, will start to feel both validated and a part of something larger. With this enhanced group dynamic, you can then transition into the second half of the workshop, in which

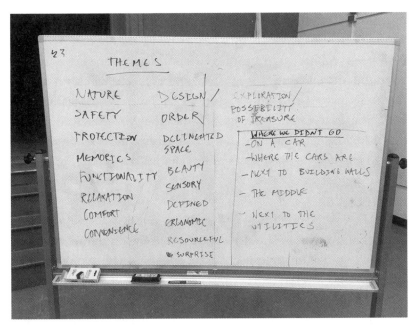

2-4. *Recurring themes that emerged from a site-exploration and model-building workshop we led with teachers from Rosewood Urban Planning and Design Magnet School in West Hollywood, California.*

participants will work in teams of no more than six to build a larger model.

The easiest way to form the teams is simply by table, as then there is no need to shuffle people around. However, if participants are gathered around one large table, simply group people together based on proximity to others. Then have the participants clear off their models from the first exercise and push their construction-paper bases together to create a larger rectangular base for the model they will build together.

The prompt for this exercise will vary based on the focus of the overall meeting, but the general idea is to move away from the self and toward the group, to collectively envision an ideal city, system, or place; build a user-centered transit system; build a more equitable city; build an LGBTQ-friendly city; build your ideal park or downtown; build a climate-resilient city. Whatever the prompt, participants will have 10 minutes to build the model, and then each team will have two minutes to report back to the larger group. As in the first exercise, it is ideal to have everyone stand up during the presentations and gather around each model while team members explain to the broader group what they've built. And similar to the first exercise, we like to follow each mini-presentation with "Let's hear it for ———" and a summary of the model, and have folks clap.

REFLECTION, DISCUSSION, AND NEXT STEPS

The second exercise should always be followed by an adequate amount of reflection and discussion. While it is tempting to simply wrap up once everyone has presented their ideas for their second model, plan ahead so that you have the time (at least 10 minutes) to lead participants through the closing of the learning and engagement process. This more extended reflection is crucial, as this is typically the stage during which participants start to make connections between the workshop and their everyday lives and surroundings; they begin to see how they could *shape* or *reshape* their lives and surroundings. Absent a reflection, participants are much more likely to simply leave the workshop behind and not give a second thought to it.

To do this second reflection effectively, begin by guiding participants through a similar reflection exercise to that of the first one: have them pull out recurring themes among the larger, team-built models. Write the themes up on a white board or flip chart so that they are not simply visible to the participants but can also be seen in conjunction with the themes from the first exercise. Once you have recorded all the themes, ask participants to look at the themes from both exercises. Which ones are similar? Which ones aren't? Why are certain themes absent from the models from the second exercise but present in those from the first? Do we lose sight of some of our values we had as children as we grow older?

These are some of the potential questions you could ask, but, as always, you may feel free to add more or modify them based on the overall theme of the workshop and the makeup of the group. Either way, make sure to give participants adequate time to respond. (It is very common for facilitators to think that a pause after a question they have asked is much longer than how it actually feels to participants.)

After discussing the aforementioned questions, another series of questions might explore what was not built. This can be too open-ended a question on its own, so adding in some examples can get the wheels turning in people's minds. Did anyone build a city full of screens (i.e., computers, smart phones, tablets)? Did anyone build a parking lot? Invariably the answers will be No, and thus this can be a lead-in to a why question: Why didn't we build so many of the things that are a part of our everyday lives? In a workshop we did with college students at Soka University in Southern California, not one student built screens or Wi-Fi or cell phone charging stations into their ideal cities, and yet all of these things are a part of their everyday lives. Having the students reflect on this discrepancy was a lightbulb moment for many of them, as they realized that when push actually came to shove, screens were perhaps not what mattered to them most in their lives and, well, if they had to, they could do without them.

Next we like to bring the exercise closer to home: How much, if at all, has this workshop changed the way you might see your every-day surroundings? How might you weave this workshop technique into your professional work or your everyday life? The underlying idea behind these questions is to encourage the workshop-goers to see the workshop experience not as one that exists in isolation and independent of their lives, values, and dreams, but as one that is a product of and can shape those lives, values, and dreams.

Finally, once you have allowed participants enough time to respond and reflect, go over the next steps in the overall process. This could mean simply explaining how the responses from the

workshop will be woven into an ultimate series of design recommendations; it could mean mentioning the next community-
engagement meeting, if this workshop is part of a longer-term
project; or it could mean simply providing your contact information in the event that participants have additional ideas, feedback,
or questions. Whatever the case, make sure that participants know
that the conversation does not need to promptly end when the
workshop ends.

SAMPLE BREAKDOWN OF THE WORKSHOP FLOW AND ALLOTTED TIMES
Meet-and-greet: 15 minutes
Workshop overview: 5 minutes
Participants build their models: 10 minutes
Participants report back on what they've built: 10 minutes
Participants draw out recurring themes: 5 minutes
Participants form into teams and build group models: 10 minutes
Teams report back on what they've built: 10 minutes
Participants draw out recurring themes, close the learning loop:
    10 minutes
Next steps: 5 minutes
Cleanup: 15 minutes

While keeping the workshop on time and on track is important,
understand that there will likely be spillover simply because of the
nature of the workshop. As mentioned, allowing people to settle
in and socialize is key to setting up an atmosphere in which people feel comfortable being creative and being creative with others.
So avoid cutting to the chase too much at the front end. And at
the tail end, factor in some extra time for conversations and connections that may have emerged out of the activities, and some
time for cleanup. "At a conventional planning meeting with simply
a PowerPoint, you can end the meeting promptly and not have to
worry about cleanup," said Karp. "So you need to be clear with the
client that this kind of workshop will require extra time, especially

at the end. Sometimes we have to send pictures of past workshops to clients just so that they understand what the Place It! method is and why we'll either need a janitor at the end or extra time to do the cleanup ourselves."

What If No One Wants to Participate in the Workshop?

Out of the hundreds of Place It! workshops we have led, we have rarely come across someone who refuses to participate. If you provide the proper background and context as to why you are conducting the workshop in a more interactive and less formal way and using found objects, and if you create a space that feels comfortable and safe enough, most people will be on board. However, there can occasionally be pushback, especially if someone has been used to always working "by the book" or is at the meeting with a particular issue or complaint they want addressed.

Says Karp on the matter and how her firm approaches things, "In particularly fraught projects, it's important to have a few people in the room who know what is going to happen and who can then engage in the exercise. Make sure you have some trusted leaders within the community and talk to them beforehand: 'Hey, we're going to do something different and inclusive, and we'll need to you step up and engage with the materials.'" In other words, their engagement will ensure that the group as a whole engages. Having this conversation well before the workshop so that key people (including the client) are on board going into it will ensure a more positive outcome. However, if there are folks who have particular grievances to be aired out and feel that these issues will not be addressed through the workshop format, you can always set aside staff to be able to address those participants individually. Karp suggests that organizers of Place It! workshops ask themselves when in the planning stages, "How do you deal in real time with one or two naysayers so that you can still move the group forward?" In other words, plan for that eventuality, but don't expect it, as most likely it will not happen if you have done the right prep work.

Place It! Method Type 2: Pop-up Models

No matter how interactive a public meeting, it is still a meeting, and it is still something people need to take time out of their day or night to attend. Given this reality, we knew early on that, in order to capture audiences who would otherwise be disinclined or unable to attend a model-building workshop, we needed to create an engagement medium that was just as interactive and creative as the model-building workshops but could bring in an unreached audience.

That need led to the creation of our pop-up model as an engagement tool. Originally, the pop-model had begun as an artistic medium that we used in creating installations in galleries and art spaces, yet we realized that it could just as easily be brought out to communities and neighborhoods to engage residents and spark their ideas for a better neighborhood. And given the larger size of the model, we could also provide a broad, physical overview of a project area in question, so that people could use their hands to build at the project scale as opposed to a small, individualized scale.

We have since built pop-up models to engage broad swaths of the public, young and old, in the design and planning of their communities and neighborhoods. And given the medium's inherent portability, we've engaged folks in a surprising array of places: outside laundromats in the Bronx; at Latino grocery stores in Eugene, Oregon; and at Compton City Hall in Compton, California (see fig. 2-5). Additionally, we have observed a side benefit of the medium: the models, by virtue of their size, color, and tactile nature, automatically draw in those who are visual, spatial, and creative in their thinking—the very folks who might otherwise shy away from attending and speaking at a public meeting.

Pop-up Model How-tos

The standard size for a larger pop-up-style model is 6' × 2.5', so it can fit atop a standard fold-up table. The base should be made of a material that is lightweight but sturdy enough to handle being

2-5. Residents of Compton, California, build their ideas for a redesigned Blue Line Metro Rail station in their neighborhood.

transported and built upon—foamcore is an easy-to-procure option (however, we will admit, it's not the greenest when it comes to disposal afterwards). Onto the base we lay a street pattern based on the project area in question (see fig. 2-6). These streets can easily be represented by strips of construction paper, which are simply glued onto the base. Primary thoroughfares should be labeled, but it is not always necessary or possible to include and label every street—especially for larger project areas—as it is important that participants not get too hung up on what already exists at that particular location in the real world. If the space in question is a park, key natural features such as streams or other bodies of water should be included, but their size need not be exactly to scale (see fig. 2-7). Again, the objective here is for people to understand what the space is but not to feel completely constrained by existing conditions. Finally, the scale should be large enough so that objects of a range of sizes can be placed within the resulting blocks and participants don't feel constrained in what they can build.

2-6. *The core framework of a pop-up model can be made out of simple materials such as foamcore and construction paper. Primary streets can be labeled to help passers-by orient themselves within the model.*

2-7. *Key natural features such as waterways and parks can be created with simple materials such as mylar or construction paper. The forms of the features need not be exact, just close enough so that passers-by can recognize them.*

Breaking Free from Perfect Scale

The looser, less exact nature of the pop-up can at times be difficult for planners and design professionals to wrap their heads around, as we are trained to favor perfect scale in models and drawings and to use these models and drawings to engage the public in the design of their neighborhoods. While this more exact approach is indeed necessary for honing one's design chops and generating more-detailed design and construction documents, it can actually be an impediment when trying to generate meaningful community input from a range of constituents.

To many who do not work in planning or design, a perfect, to-scale model can look either confusing or simply meaningless. As a result, there can then be a tendency on the part of planners and designers to want to *train* the public in understanding how to read and interpret to-scale models and drawings. However, the public's less-than-magnetic relationship to the perfect, to-scale model stems less from a lack of knowledge and much more from the simple fact that people respond to and experience cities through their senses and emotions. So then it should come as no surprise that, when it comes to talking about their cities and what they do and do not like, what they want to see changed, and what they want to see preserved, many people are often not interested in talking about zoning, setbacks, side yards, or other technical and purely physical aspects of the city that a to-scale model is trying to convey. Instead, they want to talk about places and spaces in which they do or do not feel comfortable, places that mean something to them, and places in which they feel they belong—or don't belong. The perfect, to-scale model, with all its up-to-date zoning woven throughout, can thus simply appear to much of the public as a foreign object that just doesn't accurately capture the city that people know and experience every day.

––––––

In 2018, Place It! was invited to co-lead a workshop in Santa Monica on a potential rezoning of the stretch of Pico Boulevard located within the Pico District, a historically Black neighborhood that was partially destroyed in the 1960s when the Santa Monica Freeway was built. It is one of the least affluent neighborhoods in Santa Monica, and its residents have often felt underrepresented in the planning process. During the workshop, the City handled the discussion of zoning and how it works, while the Place It! team really tried to avoid talking about technical aspects of the neighborhood and instead focused on two model-building activities: 1. Build your favorite childhood memory; and 2. Build your ideal Pico Boulevard. For the second exercise, we had made simple 3' × 2' basemaps of foamcore and then pasted a basic grid of streets on top—one street down the middle to represent Pico and two intersecting cross streets (see fig. 2-8). The names of the cross streets were not specified but were there simply to loosely match the basic form of the street pattern along Pico. Participants then picked from a range of found objects (hair rollers, fake flowers, Lego bricks, blocks) to represent what they wanted to see along the boulevard.

While some participants indeed brought up the height of buildings when discussing the models they had built, many focused simply on creating a Pico Boulevard where they felt comfortable and safe, and where they belonged. In other words, they focused on the emotional language of their city as opposed to simply a technical one. One space that several participants discussed and wanted to see more of was Black hair salons and Black beauty shops. They described how they felt comfortable and empowered in these spaces, where they could be creative with their looks and feel proud of their image. Other participants focused on the overall feel and atmosphere of the boulevard that they liked and wanted to preserve: intimate, safe, inviting. They discussed certain new developments that lacked this intimacy and talked about older commercial spaces and storefronts that allowed for the kind of inviting feel that made the boulevard a welcoming space. At no point, however, did the participants attempt to build an exact, to-scale representation of what they wanted to see, with prescribed setbacks, street-frontage

2-8. Participants at a Place It! workshop in Santa Monica build their ideal Pico Boulevard on small pop-up models that approximate but don't replicate the boulevard.

widths, or, say, curb cuts for parking. The looser, representational nature of the models and building materials made it possible for them to focus instead on features and elements, and moods and atmospheres they wanted to see on the boulevard.

So Then What?

While this looser, more-open approach to model-building and community engagement can truly lead to productive, imaginative, and meaningful responses, it is important that this feedback be documented so that it can inform the planning and urban design process.

As participants at pop-up events will come and go and thus the model itself will evolve over time based on who is there and what kinds of changes they choose to make to the model, there needs to be some way to freeze those stages of the model's evolution in time. This way, the particular stages and elements of a model can be attributed to their builders and makers. Using a Post-it-and-photo approach is the easiest way to do so. Once a participant has built a portion of the model and what they would like to see in the space or neighborhood, have them describe on a Post-it what they have built and place that Post-it in front of their creation. Take a photo of the participant, their creation, and the Post-it note, and then those ideas have been recorded. New participants are then free to move or change the model to suit their own ideas, and the process is then repeated.

Finally, three to four hours is generally enough time at one place on one day to gather a useful range of information. This time frame also helps those manning the pop-up to avoid burnout, particularly if the pop-up model will be brought to other locations.

Place It! Method Type 3: Site Exploration Using Our Senses

"We're all phenomenologists in some way or another. We're responding to and observing phenomena constantly. Different parts of our being are observing them and keeping us safe as well as keeping us within a window of tolerance," says Roché Wadehra. While she is referring to the oftentimes deeply subconscious ways in which our selves are observing phenomena around us, there are ways in which we can bring our observation of phenomena to the fore so that we are "turning on our senses" in a conscious way. This is precisely what we do with site explorations using our senses. It could be a park, a parking lot, a street, or a neighborhood; whatever the place or the scale, the objective is to bring participants to and within a physical space so that they can then explore it on a multisensory level, which includes using our hearing, our sight, our sense of outdoor temperature, and our feelings of safety or a lack thereof, among others. The combination of these senses in action serves to ignite a kind of hyperawareness that can bring forth memories, stories, and creative ideas.

In fact, the generating of creative ideas can come about precisely *because* of this hyperaware state that the sensory tours bring participants into. With this approach of experiencing space with the senses, says Wadehra, "you're getting into the sensing state, and into a sense of well-being and a meditative flow state, and that is a really great place to begin to create and to tap into the creative process." As such, we typically pair site explorations with a model-building workshop afterwards, as tour participants emerge from the exercise in a sensing state and can easily segue into rethinking and redesigning the space they have just explored. This, for example, was the case with the teachers we worked with at Rosewood Elementary in West Hollywood, California, who explored their parking lot with their senses and then came back inside, and we led them through a team-based model-building workshop in which they completely redesigned the parking lot.

Experiencing urban space with our senses is also a way to tap into memories of place. Our experience of cities and place is as much one of bricks and mortar, streets and sidewalks as it is of the layers of memory we have created as we move in and out of those brick-and-mortar spaces. Those layers give spaces meaning for us, so to walk through them with one's senses attuned and with others can spark both a revisiting of those memories and a comfort with sharing them with the other participants.

Additionally, everyday humdrum spaces you've walked or driven through hundreds of times take on new meaning and significance as you see and experience them on a completely different sensory level and through the lens of your own memories of those spaces. On the sensory-based walking tour we led with South Colton residents (explored in chapter 6), one participant, Jackie, who had lived in South Colton for forty years, suddenly realized where buildings she had seen and been to as a kid actually were. "I found out where the old Wells Fargo building was," she said. "I had no idea." This unearthing of information came about precisely because the tour jogged participants' memories, and people started to share them.

Ultimately, tapping into memories and our senses adds layers to what a standard guided tour simply could not achieve. In fact, we created the method of the site exploration with our senses as a way to take the traditional guided tour and turn it on its head—to take something transactional and move it toward something more rooted in knowledge-sharing and production. So, for example, if the site exploration is at the neighborhood scale and there are stops along the way, we can guide participants toward what to look for at each stop—a disused plaza, say—but then it is up to them to explore that particular space with their senses and memory to bring their own meaning and ideas to the fore. As a result, everyone becomes an active participant in the creation and sharing of knowledge surrounding the space or site.

SITE EXPLORATION HOW-TOS

Depending on the objectives of the project, the exploration can consist of exploring one discreet space, several spaces, or stopping points within a larger project area. The site and scale of the exploration will largely depend on what the project objectives are. In the case of our having the teachers at Rosewood Elementary explore the school's parking lot with their senses, the core project objective was providing the teachers with hands-on and sensory-based tools of exploring cities and landscape that they could fold into their curriculum (which, in their case, has a focus on urban planning and design). The parking lot was easily accessible to staff and thus could serve as a simple testing ground for the site exploration as a teaching medium. In the case of our walking tour in South Colton, the project area was much larger—about half of the entire neighborhood itself—so our site exploration needed to bring residents through a sufficient cross section of that project area that they (and we) could put together a coherent mental map of the place and gather enough information on multiple aspects of the neighborhood—memories, walkability, shade and tree canopies, commercial vitality or lack thereof, sites for new housing and public space, and everyday ways in which residents were enlivening and adorning their sidewalks and parkways. As such, the site exploration consisted of about fifteen stops along an hour-and-a-half-long walk.

For those site explorations that consist of one site alone (e.g., a parking lot, campus art center, or plaza), the core prompt we give participants for exploring the space is simply: "Find somewhere within the space that you like. Spend time there and think about why you like that particular spot." However, depending on time constraints for the exercise, you can easily add in more prompts or elaborate on the existing one. In the case of exploring a street with our senses (an activity that is explored at the end of chapter 6), we gave people an extra set of questions to think about while they spent some time in their chosen spot: "What do you hear? What do you feel? What do you see? What do you smell?" Participants had small clipboards they could jot down their responses on, or they could just use the questions as guides and make a mental note of their responses.

Whatever the prompt(s), after spending time within their chosen spots for a few minutes and reflecting on them, participants gather back together, and then we go to each chosen spot, and participants explain their selections (see fig. 2-9). Once everyone has reported back, we ask the participants to reflect on the recurring themes among the various spots. This is a crucial portion of the exercise because, as in the model-building workshops, it allows participants to start making connections between what may have initially seemed like random and disparate locations within a site. These themes can then inform a subsequent model-building exercise that explores how to redesign the space.

For site explorations that consist of multiple stops along a tour of a project area or neighborhood, we tailor the selection of stops

2-9. Participants of a sensory-based site exploration at the McColl Center for Art + Innovation in Charlotte, North Carolina. They were to find a space of comfort within the grounds of the Center. Here, Grant Meacci of the City of Charlotte talks about his chosen spot.

and what will be explored based on the overall objectives of the project, while keeping in mind the likelihood that few participants will want to walk for longer than an hour or two.

In the walking tour that we crafted for a climate-resiliency plan for the City of Rialto, we knew, based on the project objectives, that we needed to explore climate hazards and climate solutions—that is, those places within the project area that exacerbated the effects of climate change (e.g., flooding, the heat-island effect, poor air quality), and those that, if somehow replicated, could serve as useful tools for mitigating the effects of climate change. We also wanted to explore the creative ways in which residents were already retrofitting their landscapes to adapt to changes that they had already been experiencing in the environment. In this way, we were as much tapping into local, on-the-ground knowledge as we were exploring infrastructure and our senses. Thus, we chose stops along a 1.5-hour route that, for example, would have participants considering how they felt standing in a completely unshaded portion of an asphalt parking lot versus standing underneath a mature Chinese elm tree at the edge of the parking lot. This exercise would then serve as a springboard for talking about the heat-island effect and the role of mature trees in not just mitigating climate hazards but also creating the kinds of calm, inviting spaces that humans like to reside within.

Regardless of the objectives of the project, we always leave ample room for participants to share stories or memories of particular places we pass through. This is a crucial component of what Wadehra described as getting into that "sensing state," because sharing memories in a place becomes a kind of free association with the surroundings, and people start to reflect back on their own lives and how they moved within these spaces when they were younger.

At the end of the tour, we like to do a very short exercise in which participants scan back on some of the recurring themes of the ideas and memories that emerged throughout the tour. In a similar vein as with the site-exploration exercise, it is important for participants to see commonalities among what still might seem like disparate ideas and memories.

A model-building workshop following the walking tour or site exploration is recommended but not required. The sensing state that participants are in at the close of the site exploration or tour lends itself perfectly to doing some kind of creative exercise in which people design and build. Walking tours obviously take more time than a simple site exploration, so it can be asking participants too much to participate in both; however, time permitting, we do recommend it.

DOCUMENTING THE EXPLORATIONS AND TOURS

As with the model-building workshops and pop-ups, the site-exploration exercise generates a combination of ideas and discoveries that emerge through both words and space. Thus, for either a site exploration or a sensory-based walking tour, documentation of both the spoken and visual nature of the event is important. However, we would recommend not relying on one person alone to both document and lead the event. Having an additional person take notes and perhaps one other to take photos is ideal, as each can then focus on creating the richest picture of what is unfolding.

In line with all documentation of our events, we not only include in our write-ups what was said but also recurring themes that emerged from the process. Ideally these will emerge by way of a guided reflection at the end of the event, but they can also be elaborated and expanded upon as you are doing the write-up of the event. These themes can serve as core guiding principles for the larger project team—especially if the write-up is going to be passed along to a design or policymaking team. Even if not every single idea that emerges from the exercise will be able to be folded into the final designs or policies, the themes still can be. Finally, if the site exploration or sensory-based tour is done as part of a larger series of engagement events, the documentation should also reflect upon what emerged that reinforced what had been heard at previous events and what emerged that was new or potentially contradicted what had been heard at previous events. In this way, you generate a more comprehensive picture of the collective values of the group, community, or neighborhood you are working with. However, we will note here that in our experience it has been rare to see ideas emerge that contradict previous ones; more common, after three or more engagement events, is to really see a clearly emerging picture of shared values.

Next Stop

While we have now led over a thousand model-building workshops around the globe, built pop-up models across the country, and led a huge array of participants in sensory-based site explorations in places ranging from urban parking lots to suburban neighborhoods, we want to zoom in on one project in particular, in the neighborhood of South Colton in Southern California. The project is particularly instructive because it spanned an entire year, employed all three of the Place It! methods, and led to designs, plans, drawings, recommended zoning changes, and development feasibility studies. While we're there, we'll also be able to explore the equally important but often overlooked intangible outcomes that can come out of such a sequence of Place It! engagement events: a public that offers up more visionary and forward-thinking ideas; an increased capacity of everyday residents to navigate the planning process and local governmental processes; an increased sense of empowerment as citizens, designers, and planners; and more (which we'll discuss further in chapter 7). Additionally, the neighborhood has a rich cultural history of both celebration, resilience, and a uniquely Latino approach to DIY urbanism. These characteristics the Place It! methods were able to bring to the fore in order to inform the final design and planning document.

Throughout the following chapters, you will be able to follow the story of the South Colton project and the neighborhood to see what unfolded through the engagement events we held, what we learned, and what we came up with to create, in the end, what we called the South Colton Livable Corridor Plan. Along the way are stopping points that show how the same engagement methods (i.e., pop-up, model-building, site exploration) can be used within different contexts and timelines, and for different objectives. Our hope is that, via a combination of the story of South Colton and the stopping points along the way, you will come to a deeper sense of the value of engaging people through their hands and senses in cities, landscape, and design, and how you yourself can weave some of these lessons and methods into your own life, work, and everyday efforts for effecting change within the landscape around you.

Chapter 3

The Heart of Engagement: Introducing South Colton

In THIS CHAPTER, WE WANT TO take you on a tour of a neighborhood and city you may have never heard of, South Colton and the city of Colton. We led a yearlong series of interactive engagement events (i.e., model-building workshop, pop-up, and sensory-based walking tour) here that ultimately led to the creation of the South Colton Livable Corridor Plan. Not all planning, design, landscape, or transportation projects will be afforded such a generous length of time for community engagement; however, the resulting breadth and depth of the engagement we conducted meant that we were able to uncover truly nuanced and layered sets of information that offer up helpful insights for projects of any scale or duration.

The place you live or the community you're working with has history that should inform your inquiry into the place and your approaches to engagement. The location of roads, thriving and less-than-thriving commercial districts, and even how people relate to their homes and landscapes, have all been influenced by historic policies. As such, in this chapter we'll anchor South Colton within the context of the region and provide a brief history of the neighborhood, so that you can get a sense of the kinds of struggles the neighborhood has faced and the unique ways in which residents have responded to those struggles—oftentimes by enhancing the urban landscape around them and thus serving as their own DIY planners and urban designers.

From there, we'll dive into talking about the South Colton Livable Corridor Plan and how we tailored our approach to hands-on and sensory-based engagement. Our engagement strategy was guided by the desire to generate the richest amount of information possible in order to create a final plan that would be a truly unique product of the neighborhood, its residents, their struggles and ingenuity, and their hopes and dreams for a greener, safer, more walkable and vibrant neighborhood.

Considering the Region

The city of Colton, about sixty miles east of Los Angeles, is located within Southern California's Inland Empire, a region that roughly encompasses San Bernardino and Riverside Counties. The Inland Empire has never held the same status that Los Angeles has in the public imagination, or been the grist of so much cultural lore. "If you wanted to pick a defining symbol [of Inland Southern California], it would be hard to do so," says Douglas McCulloh, an artist and senior curator at the California Museum of Photography, part of the University of California, Riverside. "Perhaps a stucco tract home? Pick any of 10,000. They're fairly interchangeable."[1]

Once a patchwork of mostly small towns, the region owes its initial growth and prosperity to the citrus industry and the Southern Pacific Railroad, which not only strung towns like Colton together but also connected them to Los Angeles to the west and, more importantly, the rest of the United States to the east. Colton became incorporated in 1887, in large part because of these industries and their ability to connect what had been a small settlement to a larger economic engine.

Yet like the milling and shipping towns of New England and the once-booming industrial cities of the Midwest, when the citrus and railroad industries waned, so did Colton's—and the region's—prosperity. This decline also coincided with, and was caused by, the region's ever-worsening air quality. As Los Angeles grew rapidly in the postwar era, the Inland Empire became the unlucky recipient of Los Angeles's exhaust: the San Bernardino Mountains to the northeast and the San Jacinto Mountains to the southeast effectively create a geological bowl, the perfect pooling spot for capturing and collecting virtually all of the air pollution from Los Angeles. Now both Riverside and San Bernardino Counties have the worst air quality in the entire country.

Of course, it would be unfair and completely oversimplified to paint the region as nothing but smog and struggle. Four and a half million people live there, go about their lives, and work to make a go of things. Its population is increasingly culturally diverse, with nearly a fifth of all residents foreign born. And as Los Angeles and environs become more and more unaffordable, the region is seeing a surge in new residents, including numerous artists seeking affordable space to work. A landmark 2019 exhibition at the Riverside Art Museum entitled "In the Sunshine of Neglect" explored the ways in which the region has long served as a vast canvas for artists to explore its overlooked and seemingly insignificant spaces and the residents who inhabit and make them their own.

Set within this sprawling, turbulent backdrop, the neighborhood of South Colton is a characteristic example of the ways in which residents have worked to creatively and resourcefully improve their environment in the face of odds greater than those confronting more prosperous regions of the country. The residents' efforts and accomplishments are all the more notable given the fact that South Colton has borne the brunt of years of social and physical isolation from Colton proper (see fig. 3-1).

3-1. The southern entrance into South Colton and a plaza that has seen better days. This was one of the spaces that residents got to help rethink and redesign through our community engagement work with them.

Considering Physical and Political Divisions

The city of Colton is currently divided roughly in half by way of the Interstate 10 freeway and a now-elevated freight rail line, both of which run east–west through the city (see figs. 3-2 and 3-3). While in the past there were several physical connections between the two areas of the city, only one north–south street, La Cadena, now connects South Colton to Colton proper. Seventh Street, once called the "Broadway of South Colton" when it was the commercial and pedestrian spine of the neighborhood, effectively became a dead end when the I-10 freeway was built in the 1960s. Adding to the neighborhood's physical isolation are a spur rail line to the west and the remnant of one to the east. More recently, La Cadena, which replaced Seventh Street as the default main street of the neighborhood, was widened and designated a trucking route, with on-street parking completely removed (see fig. 3-4). Once a neighborhood of vibrant pedestrian and commercial activity, South Colton has

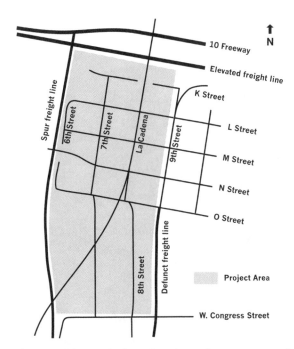

3-2. A map of the neighborhood of South Colton. The project area for the South Colton Livable Corridor Plan is shown as the shaded area.

3-3. The elevated freight rail line, which runs along the Interstate 10 freeway and almost entirely cuts off South Colton from the rest of the city to the north.

3-4. *Aerial view of the neighborhood looking north and showing the freeway-like quality of La Cadena, the neighborhood's main street. In the upper left is Seventh Street. Once a vibrant commercial street dubbed "The Broadway of South Colton," it is now completely cut off from the rest of the city to the north.*

effectively been penned in and cut off by these barriers, contributing to an environment in which commercial life is sparse and, as longtime (seventy-two-year) resident Adrian Chavez said, "Everybody drives, even if it's just one block. Nobody walks."

Widespread segregationist policies added to the historical separation of South Colton from the rest of the city. Mexicans and Mexican Americans were not allowed to own property outside of South Colton until 1952.[2] However, the segregationist policies extended well beyond housing alone. Longtime South Colton resident Alfonso Hok-Lee Garcia recalls when he and his friends could not swim in the municipal pools in North Colton, and thus a South

Colton resident, Juan Caldera, built a swimming pool for those in South Colton. Theaters in North Colton only allowed Mexican and Mexican Americans to sit on the left-hand side and not with White patrons; a curfew was in place that required South Colton residents to leave North Colton by 8:00 p.m.; and businesses in North Colton oftentimes had signs in their windows that said "White Trade Only." While these policies are long gone, there is a lingering sense within the neighborhood that it does not have or have access to the kinds of amenities that neighboring cities do.

Despite these innumerable cultural, political, and physical barriers created around South Colton, the neighborhood has long been a hub of what we would describe in modern-day terms as resiliency. Early residents of South Colton built their own homes out of disassembled wooden crates from shipments that would come through on the railroad. The neighborhood also developed into a thriving commercial, social, and cultural hub. Writes Dr. Tom Rivera, professor emeritus at California State University, San Bernardino: "We had our own churches, schools, grocery stores, a bakery, barber shops, gas stations, a furniture store, a shoe store, liquor stores, night clubs, a dance hall, and even a bullring."

Considering Unique Elements of Place

Additionally, these businesses and public facilities were (and still are) set within a physical environment that is somewhat distinct from its surroundings. The street grid and pattern are considerably less regular than within the surrounding neighborhoods. Some streets are also much narrower, with wide, generous sidewalks and parkways. Lot sizes and setbacks vary from block to block and sometimes within blocks, and commercial and institutional uses— old commercial storefronts, churches, and banquet halls—are dotted within the residential streets (see fig. 3-5).

More recently, residents have taken to adorning their generous parkways with benches, play equipment for kids, plants of

3-5. *Vestiges of a mixed-use past: small-scale commercial buildings are dotted throughout the residential portions of South Colton, giving it both a small-town feel but also speaking to new opportunities for local micro-businesses and artisans to set up shop in the neighborhood and create new economic, cultural, and artistic vitality there.*

all varieties, and large shade trees (see fig. 3-6). Some have even installed basketball hoops in the street. These DIY interventions have effectively helped to transform some of the streets into extensions of the sidewalk. Ultimately, both the resourcefulness of the residents and the separate nature of the neighborhood have allowed it to grow and evolve in a way that feels much more organic and akin to a small town than the more regular, gridded adjacent areas, where the uses are clearly defined and separated (i.e., commercial on certain streets, residential on others).

The South Colton Livable Corridor Project
In the spring of 2018, the Southern California Association of Governments (SCAG) put out a bid (or, in planning speak, a request for proposal [RFP]) for teams to submit proposals for conducting

3-6. Residents have improvised in their parkways to make the spaces usable, green, comfortable, and playful.

community outreach and research within the neighborhood of South Colton. The expectation was that from that outreach and research the chosen team would produce plans, drawings, and proposals that could help stitch South Colton back in with the rest of the city and also enhance the livability, economic vitality, and pedestrian environment for all South Colton residents. The bid had come about in part because the council member representing South Colton, Dr. Luis Gonzalez, had said he would not support a design overlay for downtown Colton without the city's support for something similar in South Colton. "I said, 'I will not sign off on the [Downtown Colton plan], I refuse to sign off on this or offer any public support unless you include South Colton on this.' And the Planning Department assured me that they were going to go after a grant for South Colton," he recalls.

Upon hearing about the bid, Gaurav Srivastava, senior urban design project manager at the planning and engineering firm Dudek, assembled a team comprising planners and urban designers from

Dudek, a market analyst, and ourselves, John and James. "When I read the [South Colton] RFP, I just knew that I had to reach out to James because it was a good fit with what he does. James came with his own set of ideas, accomplishments, and renown of just being able to work within this particular context," says Srivastava.

To prepare for the proposal, both Srivastava and James spent extensive time in South Colton, walking the streets, taking photos, and uncovering the layers of a unique neighborhood—physically, historically, and culturally. We also crafted a proposed community outreach strategy that was clear in its intention to avoid traditional engagement methods of town-hall-style info sessions or soliciting written and verbal comments from attendees. Instead we proposed our core set of engagement methods—model-building workshop, pop-up, sensory-based walking tour—in a clear effort to help bring participants' memories of place to the fore and give the residents opportunities to be visionary and imaginative about their neighborhood. The proposal the team ultimately submitted ended up being the winning one—an outcome that, at our initial meeting with Colton city staff upon beginning the project, both the city manager and planning director attributed to Srivastava's and James's extensive on-the ground-research, James's expertise in Latino urbanism, and our hands-on, sensory-based engagement strategy. The staff knew that the unique nature and history of the neighborhood demanded an equally unique approach to the project.

When we then sat down to further refine both the engagement strategy and how we would approach the design and market analysis, we knew that we needed to tread lightly and only, if and when the time came, craft bolder changes if the site or neighborhood absolutely needed it. As Srivastava recalls, "[We had to figure out] how to work in a place that has such a strong sense of physical identity and ownership of place, and to be pretty slight—to bring a very soft touch to planning in that context." This approach strayed considerably from the more typical one of bold and showy interventions and the promise of streets radically made over.

There are actually innumerable cards stacked against being slight and nuanced with a planning and design proposal. To stand out in a crowd of endless applicants for a project often encourages a "bolder is better" approach. By the same token, if the proposed design and planning approach is slight, it begs the question of why the team was hired in the first place. Additionally, planners and design professionals work within a heavily market-driven system, and thus large interventions in the private realm in the form of private developments can often dominate a planning or design strategy. Finally, there is a tendency within both the public planning and private consulting worlds to rely on tried-but-true approaches—including both strategies for engagement and the kinds of plans and design strategies that are ultimately proposed. As a result, the fine-grained details of neighborhood context, culture, and history are often overlooked. And this is a vicious circle: the more boilerplate the outreach, the less fine-grained the findings, and the more boilerplate the design and planning proposals.

In our case, given South Colton's history of separation from the rest of the city, and coupled with the ongoing efforts of the residents to better their neighborhood despite all odds, we knew that we couldn't take that generic approach; that would have been a complete disservice to the neighborhood. Instead, we sought to craft a tailored engagement plan and approach to market analysis and urban design that tapped into residents' memories and knowledge of their neighborhood, their sensory experiences of place, and their inner design and planning sensibilities and know-how.

The Role of Culture in Shaping Modes of Communication and Creation

In crafting our outreach strategy, we wanted to make sure that the spoken word was not the sole means of communicating ideas—not simply because of our knowledge of the limitations of language as a primary medium of community engagement but also because of the Mexican and Latino heritage of South Colton. In Latin American cultures and cities, and within American Latino neighborhoods, visual communication often plays a heightened role in everyday life. This important role of visual communication traces back to the colonization of Latin America, during which a language barrier meant that ideas often had to be conveyed through visual means. While at the time, the visual communication served as a means of subjugation of one culture by another, the tradition of favoring the image just as much if not more than the word has lived on and has become the hallmark of Latino neighborhoods across the United States. Murals abound, painted storefront signs with colorful, oversized images of what one can buy inside—such as toothpaste or laundry detergent—are quite common (see fig. 3-7), and in places like East Los Angeles and Barrio Logan in San Diego, there is even an architectural style that emerged during the Chicano movement in the late 1960s that could loosely be described as Chicano Modern. Taking cues from Aztec architecture, folding in murals to tell stories, and all the while embodying the modernist spirit of the age, these buildings are unique and distinctly the result of a hybrid culture that places great value on storytelling and the making of meaning through visuals (see fig. 3-8).

Yet no matter the cultural mix of the neighborhood, it goes without saying that culturally informed variations in communication vary across the United States from region to region, state to state, and even within towns and cities themselves. In Minnesota, for example, direct conflict is often avoided and language can become intensely coded so as to convey meaning and disagreement without coming across as overtly confrontational. In everyday language, we could call this being passive-aggressive; and indeed, this can be a real and negative manifestation of this form of communication. However, on its positive side, and from a cultural/historical perspective, this conflict-shy way of communicating can be seen as existing to

3-7. A painted mural outside of a mini-mart in East Los Angeles advertising what is sold there. Typical of signage in many Latino neighborhoods in the United States, the signage conveys information as much through rich visual imagery as it does through words.

create a level of order and collaboration necessary for survival in a harsh climate. It is likely a response to having to spend large amounts of time indoors during the winter with others, and an inevitable result of the region's history of immigration from Scandinavia, where direct confrontation is largely frowned upon and avoided. Additionally, there is an extra cultural layer in Minnesota of placing a premium on seeing one's existence and worth not as a stand-out individual but as part of the group—the unwritten code of *Jantelagen*, as it is known in Swedish.

Keeping these cultural quirks in mind, a tailored engagement strategy could prioritize those methods that allow people to comfortably express ideas without creating a sense of overt conflict— that is, hands-on, play-based, and sensory-based as opposed to

3-8. An example in San Diego of what we will call Chicano Modern: a rich merging of culturally informed visual imagery, American-style infrastructure, and spaces for gathering and playing.

purely verbal—and that place all participants on a level playing field where there aren't winning ideas or losing ideas and where the stage is set for easy collaboration.

Unfortunately, planning—both as a discipline and profession— has moved too far away from these qualitative ways of exploring and understanding neighborhoods and communities. With its intense reliance on quantifiable data and its efforts to act as a scientific dis- cipline and practice as opposed to a social, physical, and sensory one, planning can often forgo exploring these very real but less tangible nuances of neighborhoods, communities, and cultures. There is irony within this trend as well, as some of the hallmarks of planning thinking and practice come less from quantitative data and more from places of emotion and the senses: Kevin Lynch and his idea of the image of the city, Grady Clay's reading of the Ameri- can city through informality and how it shapes places, and Dolores Hayden and the role of gender in shaping both the built environ- ment and our experience of that environment.

An Engagement Strategy Culturally Informed and Layered

Building off of our desire to bring the less tangible and more qualitative to the fore—notably the history and cultural makeup of South Colton—and also our knowledge of how the medium of engagement directly affects the kinds and quality of feedback and ideas that are generated, we created a set of layers that guided the ultimate engagement strategy:

I.   Allow each and every resident the chance to express their ideas in ways they are comfortable with.
II. Engage participants in ways that can tap into their memories of place, their creativity, and their capacity to dream.
III. Ensure that each engagement event captures an audience that might not have attended the other events.
IV. Highlight and further explore the ways in which residents are creatively bettering their physical environment, including looking at how culture is shaping these endeavors.
V.   Ensure that the largest number of residents can participate.

More often than not, planning processes focus on the last layer alone and assume that the path toward ensuring maximum engagement is simply to repeat the same town-hall-style engagement event multiple times at multiple locations. The logic is that the drivers of poor engagement turnout and results are time and access; yet the format itself, especially if it relies on speaking alone, will invariably skew the makeup of the people who show up and participate at those events as well as the kinds of ideas and feedback that are generated, thus leading to weak turnout, superficial information gathered, and ultimately ill-informed, unnuanced plans. Additionally, it's a simple fact that, for most people, the prospect of going to a municipal building and sitting in a room after work to listen to others just talk is, even for those who have the time, not an enticing option.

However, the opportunity to play and collaborate and be creative can transform a reluctance to attend a public meeting into something closer to eagerness. "You know, we sit around and talk all the time. People like using their hands, and no one likes going to a meeting to talk about light rail. They're like, 'Okay, we've heard that story before,'" recalls Ability 360's advocacy specialist David Carey of the model-building workshop we led with disabled residents of Phoenix (a workshop explored further in chapter 4) on designing a new light rail station. "If we had marketed it as 'Come and talk about light rail,' nobody would have shown up. But the way it was marketed, people came, on a weekend."

Keeping these considerations in mind, we prioritized layers I through IV of our engagement strategy. In our case, no event type was repeated; instead, we varied the medium of engagement as well as the day, time, and location of each event. The idea was that each format, location, and time would both capture a new audience and allow for folks to engage in the ways that they felt comfortable with and that best meshed with their communication and learning styles. For our initial event (covered in chapter 4), we planned one nighttime meeting at a community banquet hall, during which we would spend some time on introducing the project but the bulk of the time on leading participants through the model-building exercises of building their favorite childhood memory and then working in teams to build their ideal South Colton.

For those who perhaps would not have the time to attend or might not feel comfortable within such a setting, we would do one pop-up model (covered in chapter 5) in front of the local grocery store. Shopgoers could simply stop on their way in or out and build their ideas for a more walkable and thriving South Colton.

Next, to capture the on-the-ground knowledge of the residents, gain a deeper sense of the unique physical nature of the neighborhood, see how residents had worked in ways big and small to improve their environment, and to engage with the landscape through our senses, we would hold an interpretive neighborhood walking tour (covered in chapter 6) late one Saturday morning.

Finally, we would hold an informal open house (covered in chapter 7) toward the end of the project where people—including casual passers-by who hadn't formally heard about the open house—could come by and offer up feedback (by way of verbal or nonverbal means) on the preliminary designs and proposals for the final Livable Corridor Plan, which would be on display in a visually engaging and coherent way.

Next Stop

Up next is an exploration of the medium of the Place It! model-building workshop. We'll look at how we tailored it to the South Colton community in particular, how we got the word out about the event, why the medium served as an effective kick-off event for the South Colton Livable Corridor project, and what we saw, learned, and observed along the way. At the end of the chapter are four explorations into how we've applied the medium of the model-building workshop to other projects, each having a somewhat different goal: resolving conflicts between bicyclists and pedestrians and between youth and adults; training urban planning and design staff in the medium so that they can use it in their own engagement work; galvanizing participants around the design and creation of a new rail station; and training teachers so that they could use the method in their classrooms. Our hope is that no matter what your background or line of work might be, your creativity will be sparked and you'll start to think about how you can apply the model-building workshop to some of your own work and efforts to create enduring spaces and places.

Chapter 4

Hands On!

Y<small>OU CAN ORGANIZE A</small> P<small>LACE</small> I<small>T</small>!–style model-building work-shop for five people or fifty—even more if you like. The size and scope will largely depend on what you are trying to achieve with the workshop. In our case, when planning for the first engagement event for South Colton, we were aiming to create a kind of kick-off event that could engage as many people and collect as much information as possible, so we were really reaching toward the upper end of workshop size.

While we'll now take you through how we pulled that off and discuss the workshop and ideas that resulted, we want to make clear that there is real value in using the method with smaller groups, too. In fact, doing these workshops with smaller groups can allow much more time for participants to elaborate on their models and memories, and to spend more time working together on their team-based models. Even with six people around a table, building their favorite childhood memories and then building an ideal city together, you'll generate infinite layers of learning and discovery. So, in reading through our approach to a larger, kick-off style workshop, think about how you could scale the medium to both your own needs and your comfort level. Keep in mind that the core goal is to create an experience that is useful, meaningful, and engaging for both the participants and the facilitators. And yes, it should be fun, too.

The South Colton Model-Building Workshop: Timeline and Sequencing

The request for proposal (RFP) process of applying for a project, being interviewed, hearing back, and then signing the contract can last many months. Yet once the contract is signed, things tend to move very quickly. The South Colton project was no exception. After meeting with city staff and finalizing the project timeline and outreach plan at the end of September 2018, we had one month to plan and publicize the first engagement event, a model-building workshop, scheduled for October 25. While such a short turnaround time is not ideal, we had to run with what we had, and this meant literally pounding the pavement and going to every house in the neighborhood to get the word out.

GETTING THE WORD OUT

"Gaurav [Srivastava] was the first one to call me [about the project], and he asked me if I had any recommendations and if I wanted to participate," said Colton city council member Dr. Luis Gonzalez of the lead-up to the first workshop, "and I said, 'I'm all in. Whatever you want to do, just include me, because I know everybody.' I've been to every single house—every one of them." Given Dr. Gonzalez's deep connections and familiarity with the neighborhood, we literally went door to door with him and left a flyer on each resident's door, occasionally talking to residents directly if they happened to be outside.

Dr. Gonzalez and his commitment to both the neighborhood and the project were integral to the overall success of the project.

"His presence in the neighborhood and city, and his visibly lending all of his weight and political capital to the effort, were huge for us. Had he not been around, I doubt [the project] would have been as successful," said Srivastava.

In fact, when we assess the relative success of projects we have done over the years in terms of high turnout at events and positive feedback from participants, one common determinant has been whether there is a local champion involved from the get-go. In short, having a local champion of the planned engagement events invariably means better and targeted promotion of the events, and a real level of excitement among participants. In South Colton, in addition to going out with us to leave flyers on residents' doors (see fig. 4-1), Dr. Gonzalez promoted the model-building work-shop (and the subsequent engagement events) through the local newspaper he writes for, the city council, calling residents directly, and his monthly CityTalk events at a local church, where residents gather to learn about upcoming events and current issues and con-cerns in the neighborhood.

The compact size and walkable nature of the neighborhood also worked in our favor, allowing us to reach the entire neighborhood in a relatively short amount of time—in one afternoon and evening, to be precise. As Srivastava points out, with a typical project and getting the word out, "you get to 10 or 20 percent of your study area's population, and that might be [considered] successful, but with this we got to 100 percent." On top of this 100 percent satu-ration, we were also reaching out to a community that has a long history of civic engagement and pride, coupled with families that date back multiple generations.

It is also important to note that our promotion strategy relied very little on social media. While we did use these avenues to a small degree, they were very much peripheral to the overall strategy of getting the word out. Dr. Gonzalez also took a similar approach. "I didn't use social media at all to promote the events," he said. "In fact, up until recently I didn't even have a Facebook account." For anyone

4-1. The flyer we left at every resident's door in South Colton to advertise for the first model-building workshop for the South Colton Livable Corridor Plan.

who has conducted a fundraising campaign, this approach should come as no surprise. Commitment to donating money most often comes from a direct ask from someone you know personally but minimally from those who might learn of your campaign by way of social media. While in our case we were not asking people to donate money, we were asking them to donate two hours of their time. Relying on personal connections for this donation of time can be crucial, especially when the interactive nature of the workshop means it will likely be longer than a standard presentation and Q-and-A.

WHY THE MODEL-BUILDING WORKSHOP COMES FIRST

The model-building workshop was a natural starting point for the engagement process, as the medium is steeped in imagining and building a better future and also establishing a level of trust among all of the participants, including those who facilitate the event. In essence, it sets the tone for the engagement events to come and for the project itself. Not only is competition absent from the exercise, but the sharing of a memory, while a positive one, can be read as a way of sharing a kind of vulnerability with the other participants. This sharing of vulnerabilities is at the core of what ultimately solidifies friendships in the long term, while in the short term it helps establish some level of camaraderie and trust within a group.

An additional benefit of holding a model-building workshop first is that you can gather a large amount of layered, nuanced information in a short amount of time, and that information can then guide and inform the planning and shape of subsequent engagement events and the overall project. Our initial impressions of a place we are new to are often based on physical characteristics of that place; yet, as we know, places take on added meaning by way of the people who live within and move through them, and their memories of these places. We can probably all think of places that are very humdrum, infrastructure-wise, but that for us are steeped in meaning because we have rich memories of what we did within them. A sidewalk in front of a nondescript house has elevated meaning for some because that is where they spent their summer days as children, playing with friends. A derelict patch of land next to a parking lot holds special meaning for some, as that is where they once camped out when their car broke down. In fact, a city contains layer upon layer of these memories attached to spaces big and small. And it is these kinds of memories that the model-building workshop uncovers. As such, the workshop leads to a heightened and deeper understanding of that place—not simply for the project team but for the participants as well. Indeed, by the end of our model-building workshop with the residents of South Colton, the entire project team had an infinitely richer take on the neighborhood and the direction of the project.

RIGHT SIZE, RIGHT PLACE

Knowing that the workshop would perhaps have the largest turnout of any of the engagement events while also wanting to maximize turnout, we chose to hold the event at the Sombrero Banquet Hall, which is centrally located within the neighborhood and is a well-known South Colton institution. Additionally, the hall can easily accommodate large gatherings, and it has the kinds of equipment we needed already on hand—ample tables and chairs, and a sound system. In this way, we had a venue that was ready for whatever size group showed up. And given the hall's central location, residents could simply walk there, if they chose, or get there by other means easily and quickly.

INFORMATION SHARING VS. KNOWLEDGE PRODUCING

For the workshop format, we intentionally departed from the standard public meeting approach of an extended presentation by city staff and consultants and then a short activity—usually in the form of a Q-and-A—with residents. This conventional format is largely one of information sharing, which starts with the premises that a change is happening, so residents need to be educated about that change; that some change in attitude on the part of the residents will result from that education; and that once there has been a change in attitude, constructive feedback can flow forth. However, rooted within this format is the assumption that the change in attitude will indeed occur and that it will occur as the result of sharing information. While it could happen this way, it might not—especially if that shift in attitude is supposed to occur in the face of a proposed neighborhood change that residents perceive as significant or even as a threat.

Rather than try to either anticipate or force an outcome, we choose to center our workshops and meetings around the idea of producing knowledge—that is qualitative, story-based, and sensory-based knowledge—both for the project team and among the participants. Instead of establishing a transactional dynamic, the goal is to create one of collaboration. While changes in attitude may indeed result, we try not to have any desired outcomes other than to gain a deeper sense of the neighborhood's memories, dreams, aspirations, and shared values; to build group cohesion; and to set a positive tone for the project.

To these ends, the final agenda for the first South Colton workshop consisted of about ten minutes of an introductory presentation and overview of the project, including a simple to-scale model of the project area; while the remaining hour and twenty minutes we devoted to individual and team-based model-building exercises, the prompts for which were "Build your favorite childhood memory" and "Build your ideal South Colton."

As with any workshop or planned event, nerves can run high leading up to the event and upon arrival, as lingering in the back of the organizer's mind is the question of whether anyone will show up. However, nearing 6:15, people started trickling into the banquet hall, and shortly after 6:30 we had thirty-five community members there, as well as two city staff, one student translator, Srivastava, and ourselves. We intentionally left a good fifteen minutes at the front end for folks to simply settle in, have some snacks, and catch up with friends and neighbors. This slower, relaxed intro set the tone for the rest of the gathering and activities.

To further enhance that atmosphere and to make collaboration with peers easier, we arranged seating around a series of tables placed in a semi-circle, each of which sat six. In the middle of that semicircle of tables was one central table on which the found objects for the model-building exercise were placed. Easels with butcher-block paper were placed at the front of this arrangement, so that everyone could see the opening presentation and the ever-expanding notes from the model-building exercises.

After a brief overview of the purpose and scope of the project by Srivastava and Dr. Gonzalez, we dove into the first model-building exercise in which residents built a favorite childhood memory using found objects. We gave participants ten minutes to find a set of objects and then build their memory, after which we gave each participant a minute to stand up and tell the room about their memory and their model. With a group as large as thirty-five, this reporting-back portion of the exercise can take quite some time, and in a different setting and for a different audience—say, a day-time staff training that has a time limit of only an hour—we might have participants just share their memories with their tablemates and then have one or two volunteers from each table share their memories and models to a larger group. In this case, however, we both had the time and were seeking to produce as much knowledge and information as possible for both the participants and the project team. Additionally, it was important that we honor and respect the memories and feedback of each and every participant, given the neighborhood's history of being shortchanged and the time everyone had taken out of their daily lives to attend the meeting.

While some participants were initially wary of the meeting itself and the hands-on activities, the less-conventional format, the presence of bright, colorful objects in the middle of the room, and the slower pace allowed folks to settle in comfortably (see fig. 4-2). Recalls Antonio Lopez, one of the attendees who also served as a translator, "At first I was very nervous, because it was a meeting with the public, and as I mentioned, I did have some idea of how they function. One of our assignments in school was watching a planning commission meeting, and [that kind of meeting] was very tight and, like, stiff when hearing the public talking to the people up front and the people up front answering [their] questions. So I thought it was going to be like that, [but when] the meeting started, when we were talking about the [project], and once we started breaking up into different groups, it became less intimidating. I think it was comforting in a way, friendlier."

This less intimidating atmosphere that Lopez describes allowed participants to mine their memories and transform them into colorful models, which were infused with both joy and a longing for a time when the neighborhood was more thriving. One participant,

4-2. Workshop participants begin mining a large table of found objects to start the process of building their favorite childhood memories.

Larry, built a model of his grandparents' house and yard, which he used to explore and which was filled with both fruit trees and small farm animals. Another, Alma, built a model of walking to the park with her parents and siblings and being fascinated by the roses there. Another, Emily, would walk to her dad's shop and then to the corner market, where she would charge her purchases to her dad, who would then find out about the charges after the fact. Recalls Jackie, an eighty-one-year-old resident of the neighborhood, of what she built, "I remembered being at the auction in Colton. There was a very famous auction there on Valley Boulevard. My grandfather, who raised me, we used to go there for animals, ducks and pigs and everything, and I remember driving down Valley Boulevard and seeing all of these cowboys—you know, by Valley Boulevard and La Cadena—I used to see them standing all in a row, and I used to think, *My God, this is a cowboy town.* That's how I used to think about it."

Interestingly, language also figured within the memories. One participant, Dr. Sosa, built a model of the moment when she suddenly realized she spoke English. Another, Andrés, built a model of coming to South Colton from Mexico and being so astounded by how much the neighborhood reminded him of Mexico but also how everyone spoke English. "I couldn't believe it—all of these English-speaking Mexicans everywhere. Some didn't even speak Spanish!" he exclaimed.

When folks began reporting back on what they had built, clear themes began to take shape. However, it was important to allow time for the participants themselves to pull out those themes by scanning back over the notes of each person's model and memory. What emerged from their and our observations were walking, family, being outside; playing with friends; sports and also less-programmed activities; community events—either participating in them or simply observing them; belonging, freedom, safety, church, animals, ritual (e.g., always walking to the store to buy candy), and language.

From this exercise and these themes, we moved on to the second exercise, building their ideal South Colton. Participants worked in groups of about six and had fifteen minutes to gather up new model-building materials and collaborate to create their models. Lively, convivial conversations began and segued into huddles of heads and hands making new neighborhoods come to life. Many were so engrossed in the exercise that we extended the build time slightly so that everyone could have a chance to make their ideas come to life. Recalls Lopez of the building process with his tablemates, "There was a lot of storytelling when we were building stuff. Some of [my tablemates] weren't even working on the project—it was more just them talking about their childhood, and I think at some point we did say, 'Okay, let's start working on this.'"

When we finally called time and the groups began reporting back on what they had built, clear and recurring themes began to emerge: spaces for gathering and relaxing—both indoor and out—access to nature, improved walkability, fewer fences, safety, and a diverse range of thriving businesses. And trees—almost every group built a South Colton with trees and shade along most or all of the streets and within new and existing public and private spaces. Lopez's group's model was no exception. He recalls of the model, "It was like a corridor with trees on the side—like a street leading up to a plaza where you were able to bike, you were able to walk. Just very pedestrian-friendly, and leading up to a plaza where people are able to hang out and talk." (See fig. 4-3.)

In fact, we had never led a workshop in which trees figured so prominently and consistently in the groups' models. But perhaps

4-3. Antonio Lopez and his group in the process of creating their model of an ideal South Colton, which included a tree-lined corridor, ample space for walking and biking, and a plaza for gathering.

the tree theme should not have come as a surprise. Many of the participants' favorite childhood memories involved some version of walking safely and comfortably from place to place within the neighborhood. "People would walk around the neighborhood, go to the stores because they were open," engagement participant Adrian recalled of the once-vibrant commercial and pedestrian life there. "There used to be one, two, three, four, four stores—five market stores in the area, and everyone would walk to them." Now there is just one market remaining. Yet in the age of climate change, and given South Colton's badly degraded tree canopy, creating a comfortable walking environment will involve much more than just commercial destinations. South Colton is subject to oftentimes excruciating sunshine and heat in the summer, and except for some very large and impressive canopy trees, many of the neighborhood's parkways and commercial streets are completely devoid of shade (see fig. 4-4). Along La Cadena are remnants of a streetscape effort that simply was never maintained: dead or dying sycamores that have barely grown if at all, and some broken in half or gone altogether. Other streets have parkways that consist mostly of dirt and sand, with not a tree in sight.

4-4. La Cadena looking north. Huge amounts of asphalt, high traffic speeds, and virtually no shade trees make for an unpleasant walking experience—especially in the intense heat of high summer.

Translating Memories, Models, and Ideas into Aspirations and Next Steps

We recorded both the memories and the elements of the team-based models on butcher-block paper at the front of the meeting space. This approach allowed participants to take stock of and reflect on what everyone had built and also served as documentation for the project team, making a post-workshop write-up as simple and accurate as possible. Yet in taking the information back home to create a write-up for the team, we had much more than a simple set of likes and dislikes—we had a deeper sense of the memories and aspirations of a community. Said Srivastava of the information we had gathered, "That's a reservoir of research that we don't normally really tap into, or that we don't have the tools to tap into. So I think just being able to pull that out and have people verbalize those memories was just—it just set a completely different tone from Day 1—how we would engage the community, what their expectations were. More specific input that we received from the first workshop was the sense of loss about Seventh Street, which used to be their historic commercial heart. The reality is that it will never become what it was . . . but I think we tried our best to make sure that Seventh Street would somehow be able to [become once again] the welcoming community that had been lost."

This insight into the central role of Seventh Street, along with feedback on trees, walking, and spending time with others outside, served to reinforce what we had noticed from our initial findings doing on-site walks and visits with local officials and residents: the public realm matters, especially in a place like South Colton, and the health of the public realm is inextricably intertwined with the health of the neighborhood. Ultimately, this observation served to shape what the plan would focus on and emphasize. "As practitioners of urban design—and especially myself—I always have this approach that the pedestrian experience of places is the defining experience of places," said Srivastava. "What [the model-building] workshop did was completely reinforce that for us, because most of the input, the memories, oral histories of the neighborhood all had to do with walking the street, walking to the store, being free, outside, hanging out with friends, so that helped us emphasize that aspect of the plan—making sure the public realm remained that welcoming, comforting, familiar place that generations of South Colton residents have known."

Finally, given the positive reaction of the participants, we knew we were right in favoring engagement methods that allowed people to use their hands, mine memories, and tell stories. We had set a tone and expectations for the project as a whole. As such, participants could look forward to the subsequent engagement events, all of which would be interactive in nature but would tap into a different set of experiences and ways of experiencing the world.

So we began planning for the next event, a pop-up model outside of a neighborhood grocery store. (It's this activity and medium that we will be exploring in chapter 5.) More overtly building- and architecture-oriented in nature, the pop-up medium allows participants to make ideas come to life atop a large model of the neighborhood. Casual and fast-paced, it allows people to stop by for five minutes, build a little vignette of what they'd like to see in their neighborhood and then carry on with the rest of their day—a perfect dynamic for outside of a grocery store or at a booth at a street fair or conference. And because we would be setting up on the weekend, we would ideally capture an audience we hadn't captured at the model-building workshop.

Other Applications of Model-Building Workshops

As this chapter concludes, we invite you to take a look at four other ways in which we have used the model-building workshop medium in our work. Each explores how the method can be used for a different goal and tells the story of the experience of the workshop and what outcomes emerged.

I. THE MODEL-BUILDING WORKSHOP AS MEDIATION

Workshop objective: Resolve conflicts between bikes and pedestrians, youth and adults

Location: Palo Alto, California

Participants: Middle school and high school students who bicycle to school; adults who walk or bike

Project timeline: Three workshops held over the course of two months

When the California Avenue bicycle and pedestrian underpass was built beneath the Caltrain tracks in Palo Alto more than fifty years ago, it was intended to solve just one problem: send peds and bikes underground along California Avenue from one side of the tracks to the other. Its design and designers never foresaw that over the years bicycling as a means of transportation would skyrocket in Palo Alto (nearly 50 percent of Palo Alto students ride their bikes to school), an increase that has now resulted in a considerable lack of shared space for both peds and bicyclists. Perhaps inevitably, each user group came to perceive the other as a problem and, in some cases, a threat.

"We knew we had a substandard-width underpass," said Rosie Mesterhazy, coordinator of the Safe Routes to School program for the Office of Transportation in the City of Palo Alto, about what had led to bringing Place It! in. "And there had been repeated attempts to mitigate the issue such as the narrowing of the chicanes, and other low-cost treatments, but they hadn't successfully changed the community's 'othering' of who was at fault." Mesterhazy described an increasingly tense situation where older pedestrians were accusing bicyclists of "pinning them up against a wall as they rode by," and younger bicyclists accusing older pedestrians of yelling obscenities and swearing at them for not fully dismounting and walking their bikes through the underpass.

However, Mesterhazy was adamant about not attempting to

resolve the situation through a traditional town-hall-style meeting as, at the core, she wanted to not simply resolve a conflict but also generate creative ideas for moving forward and, ideally, transforming the existing infrastructure. "The idea was to try and build excitement about shared ideas for mitigating the concern. I don't think you can do that in the general town-hall-meeting format, [which] often causes people to double down once they have stated their opinion and it's been affirmed by others. It can therefore lead to less dialogue, not more." And so she contacted Place It! about bringing people together using stories and model-building to generate creative ideas and defuse an increasingly tense dynamic.

Since we knew going in that the situation had been tense, we decided to first hold separate model-building workshops, one with younger users of the underpass, and one with older ones. We also made shared bike/ped spaces in general the focus of each workshop so as to get the participants to think more broadly and not focus on just the underpass itself. As such, the prompts for the model-building exercises were "Build a memory of a mobility experience" and then, in groups, "Build an ideal shared bike/ped space."

For the first workshop, with middle school and high school students, one participant, Haley, built a model of the neighborhood of Old Palo Alto and riding around in her stroller when she was very young. Her memory spoke not simply of traveling through a place but also of the sensory experience of being outside and traveling through the landscape at a slower pace, how you notice so many more details when walking than when driving. In fact, everyone's memory was of traveling by some means other than a car, and each memory described a mobility experience that was less about getting from point A to point B and more so about the experience itself. Friends and family figured prominently in most, as did nature and a sense of exploration and freedom.

In the second workshop, with older residents of Palo Alto, one participant, Rich, built a model of his walk to and from school in New Mexico, where the sandstorms were sometimes so strong that they had to walk backwards to school. That year, his grandmother gave him ski goggles for Christmas so that he wouldn't have to walk backwards anymore. Just as in the first workshop with youth, these participants' memories had less to do with simply getting from one point to another and more with feelings of freedom and exploration, being outside, navigation, friends, and family.

The second building exercise for both the younger and older groups involved working in teams to build an ideal shared mobility space. The models that each team built had recurring themes of providing not simply ample space for bicycles and pedestrians traveling at varying speeds but also space to simply hang out with friends, play a game, or relax with family. In other words, the spaces allowed for people to get from point A to point B but didn't make that the sole purpose. And in each model, cars were relegated to a much less prominent role within the space than what we currently have in our actual infrastructure.

For both workshops, participants were removed from any sense of threat and any attachment to an actual space and thus could let creative ideas flow forth. "Collective play," says Roché Wadehra, "is really about giving each other permission to let our guard down, of it being a safe space to explore possibility. And that really helps people feel great. They feel connected and have a sense of belonging within the place they live." In fact, establishing a sense of belonging and connection is at the core of the success of the workshops, Mesterhazy feels, and this showed each demographic that, at the end of the day, everyone wanted the same thing. "How we approach it might be different," Mesterhazy says, "but we all want the same things—communities that make us feel connected."

Having established these core values and ideas, we gathered the participants all together one month later for a subsequent workshop at the underpass itself. We started by going over the ideas from each previous workshop, so that each demographic could see the overlap in ideas and themes, and then we led the participants into a spatial and sensory-based exploration exercise within the underpass. Afterwards, we gathered back together and broke up into teams, and each built their ideal California Avenue Underpass (see fig. 4-5).

4-5. Participants of all ages were able to successfully come together to build creative ideas for a shared bike/ped California Avenue underpass in Palo Alto, California.

It is important to point out that we worked on a model-building exercise on the design of the underpass itself only after having led the participants through multiple model-building and sensory-based exercises beforehand. Had we started the entire process with a model-building exercise on the underpass itself, we would have risked running into the very conflicts we were attempting to diffuse. Instead, by the time all of the participants had come together at the end, they were able to freely generate creative and visionary ideas that would allow for a multiplicity of users to share the space.

II. City of Charlotte and the McColl Center for Art + Innovation

Workshop objective: The model-building workshop as staff and community training

Location: Charlotte, North Carolina

Participants: Staff of the City of Charlotte's Planning, Design, and Development Department

Project timeline: Place It! came in mid-project, after the North Tryon Vision Plan had been completed in 2017, but before engaging with the community to the north of the Plan area

The North Tryon neighborhood in Charlotte, North Carolina, is at the confluence of what have become hallmarks of contemporary American urban change: years of disinvestment and shortsighted redevelopment; struggling resident populations now facing sudden flows of significant investment into new development in the neighborhood; major planning and zoning changes; and the challenge of not simply inviting new residents in but lifting those longstanding ones up and ensuring that they can stay. Given the complexities of the neighborhood and the numerous changes afoot, the City of Charlotte was looking for new ways of engaging the community that could be more nuanced and inclusive.

As such, the City first invited Place It! in to lead an interactive, model-building workshop for planning staff in 2017 that centered on North Tryon. The workshop was a primer and a training, introducing planning professionals to a new method of not only doing community engagement but also visualizing place so that they could then use the method on their own when engaging with the North Tryon community. The specific model-building exercises Place It! engaged them in were building a favorite childhood memory and then working in teams to build an ideal street.

Charlotte Urban Design Center manager Grant Meacci wanted to train staff in the Place It! model-building method in part because of the accessible nature of the medium. "It's a new way, but using old techniques, and it's not intimidating," said Meacci. "It's such a nonthreatening way to engage all ages that, to me, it just needed to be spread out there, so that more people knew about it. Planners [at the training] thought it was an interesting way to talk about complex subjects without having to use jargon or get people to use maps or draw in two dimensions."

From there, Meacci built a Place It!–style pop-up model (a medium explored in chapter 5), which he had learned from James at a previous event in Raleigh in 2011. We then sent the staff a set of found objects they could use along with the pop-up model at subsequent community-engagement events in North Tryon. "This is really meant to be the basis for the ongoing conversation involving all of the different groups who are trying to make a better North Tryon," said Meacci.

Place It! was then invited back a second time, in the summer of 2018, to lead a fifteen-person workshop with diverse members of the North Tryon community (see fig. 4-6), and to train members of the McColl Center for Art + Innovation staff and members of

4-6. Meacci and a workshop participant at the McColl Center for Art + Innovation working together on a model of their ideal neighborhood.

the community in the model-building workshop method. Meacci and James also trained these same people in building the pop-up model and using the model to engage communities. "We have since created a facilitator guide, and now we'll be bringing the model out into the community," said Alli Celebron-Brown, the Center's president and CEO.

In reflecting back on the process, Celebron-Brown was struck by how the workshop medium was able to bring together otherwise disparate groups and shift balances of power. "There are always power dynamics—you can never erase that completely—but this process was one of the most level playing fields in this neighborhood's history," said Celebron-Brown. "In terms of housing and neighborhood development, it was incredible. You don't have to have experience or a title or influence in those traditional ways that are typically respected within the planning world. Everyone's ideas are valid and respected."

In speaking of next steps for the project and the media of both model-building and the pop-up, Celebron-Brown said, "We're also working on identifying nonprofit organizations, neighborhood leaders, and going deeper with the partners we've worked with—city, county, men's shelter—and then we're taking Place It! to them or bringing them [to the McColl Center] to bring more people into the process, to gather more data, and ideally to validate some of the assumptions we've already made through the first process, but also to help people become aware of all the changes taking place in our neighborhood."

III. Ability360

Workshop objective: The model-building workshop as means of galvanizing participants around transportation infrastructure

Location: Ability360, Phoenix, Arizona

Participants: Members of the disabled community of Phoenix

Project timeline: Idea for station emerged in 2004, when Ability360 was built; one Place It! workshop held in 2013; funding secured in 2015; project broke ground in 2016; station opened in 2019

In 2013, Place It! facilitated a model-building workshop with disabled individuals who wanted rail access to the recently built, state-of-art Ability360 Center in Phoenix, Arizona, which serves as a regional community center for Phoenix's disabled community and which contains the offices of ten nonprofits as well as gym facilities, multiple pools, meeting rooms, and a running track, among other amenities.

In the immediate years following the completion of the center, getting there was no easy task. While the facility was adjacent to an existing light-rail line, the nearest stations were a mile away in either direction. For many who went to Ability360, driving was not an option, so they had to rely on their parents or a relative to drive them, or a van carrier or a city bus (and given the sprawling nature of the Phoenix region, many would have to make multiple transfers, a task doubly complicated if they required wheelchair assistance).

While some planners and policymakers tout buses as a cheaper, more easily implemented alternative to light rail, the center's advocacy specialist, David Carey, makes clear that for many disabled residents, a bus is simply not an option—especially in the oftentimes punishing summer heat of Phoenix. "No one wants to catch a bus—three buses to get there, three buses back. No one wants to wait at a bus stop in 116-degree heat just to go swimming [at Ability360]. You'd be dead by the time you got there."

While the idea for a station really emerged when Ability360 broke ground in 2004, it took years to generate enough political support for the project. When it became increasingly likely that funding the station would be a reality—in particular when then-mayor Greg Stanton became a firm advocate for the project—Ability360 brought in Place It! in 2013 to lead folks in a model-building workshop on designing their ideal light-rail station.

Though held on a Saturday, the workshop was well attended, which Carey attributes to the hands-on nature of the workshop. "You know, we sit around and talk all the time. People like using their hands, and no one likes going to a meeting to talk about light rail. They're like, 'Okay, we've heard that story before.' If we had marketed it as 'Come and talk about light rail,' nobody would have shown up. But the way it was marketed, people came—on a weekend."

The workshop participants not only built models that brimmed with extremely creative ideas (see fig. 4-7), but the event also served as a galvanizing force for increased grassroots support for the station. "Some people had great, far-out ideas, like everyone does. Some people said, 'I want waterfalls. I want elevators.' But that's the whole purpose of this kind of thing—you kind of throw

4-7. Participants in the workshop at Ability360 in Phoenix, Arizona, build a model of their ideal light-rail station. Many of their ideas were subsequently woven into the design of the actual light-rail station, which was unveiled in 2019.

out ideas and get people excited about the project. Getting them excited about something will get them involved and want to advocate for [the station]," said Carey. "The disabled community had been asking for a station for years, and so with that said, [the workshop] got people thinking, 'Oh, this could really happen.'"

After the workshop were two years of further lobbying and advocacy for the project, which ultimately led to Mayor Stanton requesting a feasibility study of putting in a new station within an existing rail line. To Carey's surprise, the two most conservative members of the Phoenix city council voted in favor of the study, and funding for the station project was secured several months later. The project then broke ground in 2016.

When the station opened in 2019, workshop participants were able to see many of the ideas they had built in their models come to life. The station has trees and shade, wide sidewalks, heat-sensitive lighting (if you move near it, it turns on), and even a waterfall. And everything is at street level so that no elevators are required. Carey says that the at-grade nature of the design and the extensive shade are core components of what makes the station design successful.

However, beyond these physical elements of the station, Carey says the station provides those who frequent Ability360 with a level of freedom and independence they simply did not have before. "They don't have to rely on Mom and Dad or a carrier to bring them there," said Carey. "And instead of it taking you three hours to get there [on a bus], you get there in twenty-five minutes or thirty minutes from where you live without ever having to transfer and never needing assistance getting on and off the trains." While he has heard that some still cannot take light rail because of a lack of a station close to where they live, he emphasizes that the addition of the station next to Ability360 is part of a much larger process. "The light rail is not one and done. It's continuing to expand to different parts of town. You can be short-sighted and say it's not going to my street, but it's going to eventually go to different parts of town through expansion."

IV. Rosewood Elementary School

Workshop objective: The model-building workshop as a teaching method

Location: Rosewood Elementary Urban Planning and Design Magnet School, West Hollywood, California

Participants: Grades K–5, students and teachers

Project timeline: Third in a three-day series: Day 1. Training for teachers in model-building workshops; Day 2. Training for teachers in sensory-based explorations of space; Day 3. Daylong series of model-building workshops for students

Rosewood School in West Hollywood is not your typical public school. An urban planning and design magnet school, its curriculum not only has a STEAM (science, technology, engineering, art, and math) focus but also works to foster a new generation of great city thinkers, builders, and problem-solvers. And, perhaps unexpectedly, it is a K–5 school—kindergarten through fifth grade.

In the winter and spring of 2019, Rosewood invited us to conduct two afternoons of trainings and workshops for teachers and then a daylong series of interactive model-building workshops with students of all ages. While our approach varied somewhat from class to class depending on the age of the students, what we first and foremost wanted to accomplish with the students was to introduce them, in simple terms, to what urban planning is and then have them build models of their favorite and most cherished parts of their cities and what they love to do there.

What was most instructive to observe and learn was how the students' conceptions of both urban planning and cities evolved over the course of the short, forty-five-minute workshops.

"What is urban planning?" we would start off by asking.

"Buildings!" many of the students would eagerly reply.

"What does an urban planner do?"

"Designs buildings!" they'd say.

"How does a planner know what to design?"

"He just knows how to design buildings!" one student would offer.

Across age levels, the students initially understood urban planning and cities as mainly consisting of static infrastructure separate from their everyday lives. Yet when we then introduced the model-building exercise of having them build what they loved to do in cities—their favorite activity, their favorite place or spot—the students created cities that were much more than mere buildings, and they began to see how planning both shapes and is shaped by their lives.

As a bridge to that activity, we talked about the last question, "How does a planner know what to design?," in very simple terms: planners have to know how people live and what their lives are, what they love and like and do, before they can plan. "So we're going to build what we love to do in cities so that we can then plan our cities better."

Eagerly running to one of two tables set at each end of the room that were piled up with trinkets and found objects, the kids had mini treasure troves of colorful objects to pick from. Before building, one third-grade boy had eagerly said, "I'm going to build a video game system!" This was perfectly fine and within the purview of what they could build, as we left the prompt very open-ended. However, when the student started building with his found objects, he created something quite different from what he had planned: a park.

In fact, during the report-back portion of the exercise, when we went around the room and had the students share what they had built, that particular student expressed complete surprise with himself at what he had made: "I said I was going to build a video-game system, but I ended up building a park! I don't know why!"

His reaction speaks volumes to the ability of this method to help us mine and tap into our core values. Our lives may involve activities like video games, shopping, watching TV or movies online, parking lots, and driving. Yet when prompted to build either their favorite activity in the city or, for older participants, their favorite childhood memory, people young and old never build models of these activities. Instead, they consistently build memories or experiences that have to do with friends, family, nature, exploration, and belonging—in essence, activities that speak to what in our lives we hold near and dear.

So then where does all of this go? In the case of Rosewood, we had conducted a series of trainings on these methods with the teachers, and after the workshops, the teachers began weaving this model-building method into their everyday curriculum, regardless of subject. Christine Neil, then magnet coordinator and now a kindergarten readiness coach within the Los Angeles Unified School District, relayed that teachers had the students write about their model-building experiences. "We have worked to integrate the planning-related projects into our standards such as reading and writing. So the students journaled about what it was like to build models and learn about urban planning," said Neil.

She also offered up a glimpse of next steps for the students, beyond just reading and writing. "I would propose a civic activity in which students looked into areas in our neighborhood that might be similar to the places they built and also those places where they might put what they had built in their models," said Neil. "With the older students, I'd propose a follow-up field trip to a planning office to meet with a planner, so that they can ask those questions of planners directly. That covers social studies, oral language, and reading."

Chapter 5

Pop Up!

In MANY WAYS, THE PLACE IT! pop-up model explodes our conception of what a model city can be. The premium placed on perfect scale is thrown out the door, and loose representation of places and spaces takes its place. While to formally educated architects, planners, and designers this removal of perfect scale might seem horrifying, destined to produce unhelpful and impractical results, it's really this lack of perfect scale and perfectly true-to-life representation that allows participants to tap into their inherent wealth of creative ideas.

In fact, so many of the tools that design professionals and planners love using in their own work as a form of design inquiry and creation can actually be crippling to those well outside of those worlds and professions. "If people have to draw a map, they'll be really precious with it. If you put a pencil in people's hands, people feel like they have to be precious," said Dr. Kate Langham, creative director and co-designer of the UK-based design firm Langham Studio. Langham actually uses cake, cookies, and candy as her medium for engaging everyday people in design—including the design of parks. She's observed time and again that while participants in community-design workshops might be hesitant or overly concerned about perfection when using Legos or having to draw, they will open up and become noticeably freer in their creative thinking when working with cake, cookies, and candy as the building blocks of models. Kate also notes that hand washing is not advised until the model building is done, as she observed early on in her workshops that hand washing led to a kind of stifling and limiting of the creative imagination.

In a similar vein, the Place It! pop-up models are bold, colorful, and playful, and they are seen as durable and not precious in the least. This appearance tacitly says to passers-by that one need not be delicate with the model at all. As such, those who stop by to build can let their imaginations run wild—even if it is just for five minutes. And this is precisely what we observed in South Colton when we set up our pop-up model outside a small but much-frequented grocery store. People would come by for a few minutes, let their creativity loose, and then carry on with their shopping. Along the way, we observed how the activity invariably lifted people's spirits, and we left with a wealth of useful and meaningful information to shape and inform our design, zoning, and market approaches to a more walkable, safer, and greener South Colton.

This chapter explores that process from where the pop-up fell in the project timeline to the fabrication of the model and on to the information we uncovered, and it discusses how that information informed our design and planning inquiries. As with the previous chapters, we want to show how a medium that, at first glance, can seem like mere child's play can generate a richly layered amount of information about neighborhood aspirations, creative ideas, and a community vision.

The Pop-up as Part of a Sequence of Engagement Events

We scheduled the pop-up model event for Saturday, December 15, allowing us enough time to prepare and providing a buffer of time between this event and the model-building workshop. Holding an engagement event too close to the previous one risked us running into a kind of early engagement saturation, where we would potentially reduce interest in the event and project and also burn ourselves out in the process. Sometimes, given the short timelines of many projects, this is not possible, but here we had the time, so we chose to take it.

Scheduling the pop-up event on a Saturday was very deliberate, as we were trying to reach an audience we would not otherwise interact with through a weeknight meeting. The nature of a pop-up model is generally one of engaging passers-by as opposed to inviting people to come to a meeting at a set place and time. As such, you boost your chances of reaching those passers-by who have some time to spare when you schedule a pop-up event for a weekend—or, if not a weekend, then holding the event at a festival or celebration during the week, where the prevailing mood will already be relaxed and convivial. Scheduling a pop-up for a weekday evening risks minimizing how much engagement you will have, as people will invariably be more stressed and pressed for time.

THE VISUAL-LEARNER MAGNET EFFECT

Not only does the pop-up model capture an audience that might not be able to attend a longer, sit-down workshop, but it also tends to naturally draw in those who are visual and spatial in their learning styles. The models are large, colorful, and recognizably tactile, and thus they serve as their own advertisement, or as objects of conversation. As such, the format all but eliminates the need for those manning the table to yell at passers-by to come over and check out the model. In our experience, those who notice and are naturally visual learners stop and build. The result is a dynamic that lessens the pressure for not just the passers-by but also those behind the table.

Additionally, as the nature of the interactions at the model tend to be quick—people stop and build for typically no more than five minutes—you can generate a large amount of information and many ideas over a short amount of time. In our case, we planned to be set up from 10:00 a.m. to 2:30 p.m., which would ideally give us enough time to capture a broad cross section of passers-by and ideas.

Tailoring the Model to the Colton Setting and Audience

For the model itself, we laid a large, to-scale version of the street layout of the project area atop a 6' × 3' sheet of foamcore, and we labeled the streets with large lettering, all with the intention of making sure that what the model depicted was instantly recogniz-able to passers-by. However, it was important that those engaging with the model not feel constrained by what currently exists in the neighborhood, so the true-to-life nature of the model stopped there. The buildings and objects we supplied for people to build their ideas with were movable, colorful, not to-scale and not literal representations of any of the existing buildings or landscape features in South Colton. Additionally, it was equally important that passers-by not think of any of the objects as too precious or not to be touched. Using an array of colorful found objects of a range of sizes and scales, shapes and forms, thus fit the bill.

To further clarify what we were doing and to categorize people's suggestions, we set up easels to the right of the model. One simply said in large letters "Plan Colton," while the other was for putting up the Post-it notes of people's ideas (see fig. 5-1).

Choice of Location

To hold the event somewhere that would guarantee passers-by, we chose to set up outside the one grocery store within the project area, Sombrero Market. A popular spot within the neighborhood, it doubles as a lunch counter and is perhaps the one business remaining in South Colton that has a predictable volume of foot traffic through its doors throughout the day.

5-1. The set-up for the pop-up model outside of the Sombrero Market in South Colton.

GETTING THE WORD OUT

Because we were intending to engage casual shopgoers in the model rather than sit-down participants, we did less publicity for this event than for the initial model-building workshop. Dr. Gonzalez publicized the event through his networks, and we did as well. While recruiting participants ahead of time is less important with this kind of engagement, it's important to have people to help out at the table. No one person must commit for the full amount of time, but having a few people (not just one!) manning the model or around the model at all times helps create an atmosphere of curiosity and engagement that, we believe, further entices folks to stop, have a look, and build their ideas. As such, we had one student from Cal Poly Pomona, Baltazar Barrios III, with us the whole time; Dr. Gonzalez came by for an extended period, as did local resident Andrés and an architect and landscape designer who grew up nearby, Ruth Gallardo, all four of whom speak both Spanish and English so could easily converse with anyone who came to the model.

Uncovering Ideas and Aspirations

When folks approached the model, we would typically start with a very quick introduction of what we were doing and then ask them to find where they lived on the model. This served as both an icebreaker and a way for folks to orient themselves within the model. "They were curious about what was going on, and then they would realize, "Oh yeah, that's that street," recalls Gallardo of the moments when passers-by would make the connection between the model and their neighborhood. From there, we would move on to encouraging them to build their ideas by asking one or more of the following directed questions: How would they improve South Colton? What do they like about South Colton? What problems do they see in the neighborhood? While some passers-by seemed to be in a hurry, we ended up engaging with forty-five residents in total (see fig. 5-2).

From their responses and ideas, safety emerged as a particular

5-2. Shopgoers discuss and build their ideas for a reimagined South Colton.

problem people saw in the neighborhood; however, often it was safety linked more specifically to pedestrians, walkability, and comfort than to crime. As such, people's built ideas for an improved South Colton centered on improved crosswalks, slowing traffic on La Cadena, more and better pedestrian lighting, and transforming alleyways into walking corridors. Additionally, because the model captured a bird's-eye view of South Colton and adjacent neighborhoods, people could distinctly see the division and barriers between South Colton and the greater Colton community. As a result, people built in inviting walkways and corridors that would allow for those barriers to be bridged and for South Colton residents to have easy pedestrian access to nearby amenities currently physically cut off from them.

Green space also came up quite frequently. "Everyone had this desire for trees and shade, including for bus shelters," recalls Gallardo of one of the strongest recurring themes of what people built. She attributed this to both the climate of the area and the distinct lack of shade. One person at the model put in shade trees along sidewalks and suggested they be a mix of both evergreen and fruit trees and then making opportunities for fruit-picking programs for local residents and youth.

Other ideas centered on buildings, façades, and destinations. Just as at the model-building workshop, people built in a more activated South Colton in which businesses were not simply thriving but also attractive places to walk to. Residents wanted less in the way of tire shops and strip clubs and more in the way of restaurants, cafés, plazas for gathering, and a weekly night market. Additionally, they wanted to see storefront façades that were inviting and enticing to the pedestrian and not just to motorists passing through. A recurring theme that emerged and continued to emerge was that South Colton residents really wanted change; they wanted the kind of walkable, amenity-rich community that so many of us long for in the modern age of wide streets, lots of cars, and big-box stores. In fact, this has been a strong recurring theme of many of the workshops and pop-up models we do: the infrastructure we've been given doesn't square with what we value and how we want to live our lives.

Translating Ideas into Gatherable Information

After building their ideas, participants would write down the general themes of their creations on Post-it notes and place the notes next to their creations. We would then take a picture of at least the Post-it note and what the person had built, or, if they were okay with this, a picture of the participant next to what they had built and the Post-it-note description. From these photos, we were able to go back and create a write-up of the specific ideas participants had come up with. We then distilled these into themes and organized them around two broad categories, "Challenges" and "Opportunities." We then relayed this write-up to Gaurav Srivastava and the project team with Dudek. (For more specific details on what emerged, see chapter 7, which explores outcomes for all of the engagement events in greater depth.)

In reflecting on the findings, Srivastava recalled a few stand-outs. "One was that [the pop-up event] reinforced what we had heard at the workshop, and again that vacant parcel [at La Cadena and O Street] was identified as a future opportunity. Some of our ideas that had to do with connecting the neighborhood to the rest of the city, like under the railroad tracks, those ideas were expressed both at the first workshop and at the pop-up model because, when seeing the physical layout of the neighborhood, one could really then talk about it, where the connections are challenged."

Where We Were in the Design/Recommendation Process

Despite gaining yet another round of extremely useful information and insights from residents, we and the Dudek team were firm about not pursuing any design plans or formal recommendations at this point. We still had the walking tour to lead in January, and concurrent with our ongoing engagement efforts was the economic and market analysis led by Lance Harris of Proforma Advisors. Harris had met with the City of Colton's director of economic development, Art Morgan; spoken to developers to get a sense of the lay of the land; and was conducting market analysis of the neighborhood through the lens of its history and physical separation from the surrounding areas. In light of this separation, he looked at what kinds of residential and mixed-use building types would be attractive to developers in the neighborhood and/or what would need to change for this kind of development to break even or create a profit. The initial conclusion: investment would most likely not come about on its own by way of a simple hands-off approach. "There's land vacancy in South Colton, and years of disinvestment," said Srivastava. "One of the ways to reverse that is you find activities and amenities and you bring those to the neighborhood, but it's physically separated by the rail corridors from hubs of retail and other economic activity, so it's in a challenged position. The other constraint is under existing policy at that time—zoning and land use—the kinds of buildings that would pencil out were disallowed." Given these realities, we knew at this point that to make some of the community's visions a reality would at least require some set of zoning changes.

WHERE to NEXT

What remained now was to get out into the neighborhood and explore it with South Colton residents. In fact, if the project you are doing engagement for centers on an actual physical space, we want to encourage you to fold in one engagement event that brings participants to the space in question (e.g., a street, a vacant lot, a parking lot, a neighborhood). It's not only a way to test some of the ideas that have emerged from the model-building workshop and/or pop-up against reality, but it can also serve as a means of generating additional layers of information and capturing an even broader audience. Additionally, you take a space from the abstract to the real. This then heightens people's awareness of that space, as participants are asked to not simply be within the space but also respond to it with their senses.

Up next, then, is a deep dive into our site exploration using our senses with the residents of South Colton. Given that the site was the neighborhood itself, one of the challenges was to craft an exploration that could paint a thorough picture of the stories, memories, and aspirations of a place but also not be so extensive as to be exhausting. We'll look at how we tried to strike that balance in the crafting of our route and then explore what stories, memories, and creative ideas emerged from the tour along the way. As most readers are probably unfamiliar with the neighborhood, we've included maps and ample visuals that, ideally, will anchor you in the place.

Before proceeding, we first invite you to look at two other ways in which we have used the pop-up model as an effective tool for community engagement that sparks people's creativity and curiosity: reaching immigrant communities through the creation of a park's master plan in Eugene, Oregon, and building young people's capacities in urban design and community engagement in Minneapolis, Minnesota.

I. Eugene Parks Master Plan Update

Workshop objective: Pop-up model as a means of reaching immigrant voices for update of parks master plan

Location: Eugene, Oregon

Participants: Latino communities in Eugene

Project timeline: Three years; pop-up used on multiple occasions throughout the project

"Latinos felt really unwelcome in [Eugene's] public spaces," recalls Gerardo Sandoval, a University of Oregon associate professor of planning, public policy, and management, of a HUD-funded study he had embarked on to explore the needs of the Latino community in Eugene. So when the City of Eugene embarked on a three-year process of updating its parks master plan, he saw an opportunity to explore how to create parks that were inviting to a diverse range of residents, including its growing Latino community.

Yet in thinking about how to uncover those solutions, Sandoval wanted the city to explore some less usual-suspect forms of information-gathering and engagement. "I wanted to do something different," he said. "Usually you bring in experts, and they bring in quantitative metrics. But the [Place It! method] leads people to talk about themselves, gets people telling stories." So through a combination of funding from the city and his own funding, he started the engagement process by bringing in James to train him and his students in building pop-up models.

For the training, James led Sandoval and his students through what materials to use, how to scale the model, how to lay out the streets, and how to document people's ideas once the pop-up is out in the field (see fig. 5-3). With the resulting models, they then went

5-3. James helps a University of Oregon student build the pop-up model they'd be using to engage residents in their ideas for the new City of Eugene parks master plan.

out into Latino communities to engage people in their ideas for a more inclusive parks system.

"We took [the model] to a lot of different places—to a Latino festival, workshops at two community-based organizations, and actually inside Latino businesses such as grocery stores. At parks as well. When the city had their Latino family night, we did [the pop-up] there," said Sandoval (see fig. 5-4). "We interacted with about 500 residents total. The students would take detailed notes, but the point was to get into a conversation with people—what is your ideal park, what would you like to see in the park? After a while, certain patterns started to emerge. My job was to see these patterns emerging so that I could make some policy recommendations to the city."

5-4. *The pop-up model at the entrance of a local Latino grocery store in Eugene, Oregon.*

One emerging pattern had to do with the city's reservation system for picnic and barbecue areas within the parks. Longtime residents had used a reservation system, but the newer Latino residents were either unaware of the system or could not use it due to limited

English skills. Additionally, there was a cultural component to the misunderstanding. "There isn't a system like this where they come from," said Sandoval. "Latinos just show up." As a result, conflicts had arisen between those who had made reservations and those who hadn't and just showed up.

To resolve these recurring conflicts, a key component of the final parks master plan was a wholesale revamping of the reservation system. Per the new plan, only Eugene's larger parks have the system, and a new bilingual employee manages the reservations. "They also developed a program called 'Park Ambassadors' who are bilingual and go up and talk to people in the parks and ask them what they would like to see," said Sandoval.

Additionally, out of one of the pop-up engagement events that Sandoval and his students did with a local junior high school emerged the idea of naming a new park after a historical Latino leader. "With [the Place It!] workshops, you never know what you're going to get. You have to come in with an open mind. This thirteen-year-old girl had this idea [for naming a park after a Latino leader], and it actually happened—it became a reality and the park is now called Rachel Ortiz Park."

Perhaps as a final added bonus of the whole process, Sandoval has now woven pop-up model-building into his urban planning history course. "When we get to the section on Ebenezer Howard and the Garden City, I actually have the students design a Garden City with [the Place It! pop-up] method," he said.

II. JUXTAPOSITION ARTS AND THE RIVER FIRST PROJECT

Project objective: Pop-up model as a means of youth capacity-building in design and community engagement

Location: Minneapolis, Minnesota

Timeline: One year: Place It! taught students how to make the pop-up model at the beginning of the project; the students then used the model throughout the duration of the project but on their own

In 2016, youth of color from the Northside district of Minneapolis, the most economically depressed area of the city, became their own urban planners and facilitators. They were at the Capri Theater with a pop-up model of the Mississippi River they had built and were asking attendees a series of questions to get them to imagine and build what they wanted to see along the banks of a neglected stretch of the Mississippi just north of downtown Minneapolis.

"We had some prompts that the kids used to have conversations with [the event-goers]: 'Do you have any memories of going to the river?' 'Have you ever touched the river?'" recalls community outreach specialist and urban designer Coal Dorius, a teacher and mentor at Juxtaposition Arts, a Minneapolis-based youth arts organization. "We made it very soft and feely. We were trying to really drive home that [in North Minneapolis] there is not a lot of connection to the river."

Some months prior, Place It! had come to Juxtaposition Arts to work with these same students on building the base pop-up model of this particular stretch of the Mississippi. The students were part of a landscape- and urban-planning-focused studio called the Envirolab, headed up by Dorius and architect Sam Ero-Phillips. The students (or "apprentices," as they are called at Juxtaposition) had actually already had a crash course in the fundamentals of urban and landscape design and were now applying those skills to City-led efforts to re-envision and ultimately revitalize a formerly industrial and now-decaying riverfront.

"We tried to take them through the whole design process—how you do a mock-up, how you do iterations, how you do a schematic design," said Dorius of the early phases of the Envirolab. "But we were doing this within the physical space of Juxta. It was really good for them to start visually understanding their space."

The Mississippi model was a chance for the students to start expanding the scale and scope of their design chops and know-how. Using large print-outs of aerial photos of the project area, we worked with the students to make a foamcore model with variations in topography and a strip of blue that loosely followed the contours of the river (see fig. 5-5). This became the model that the students later traveled with as they conducted their own community outreach on the river—going to the Parks Foundation, where it lived for a while, then to the Capri, and on to the University of Minnesota.

5-5. Students in Juxtaposition Arts' Envirolab learning how to build a pop-up model of the Mississippi River just north of downtown Minneapolis.

For many of these students, this was the first time that they were directly engaging with the public as their own public outreach specialists. (The Envirolab had prepped the students on how to talk to the public about potentially complicated planning concepts in a jargon-free way.) The model then served as an effective jumping-off point for the conversations the students would have. Rather than have the students stand up in front of a crowd and speak without any visuals or physical objects to use, they were able to use the model as context for their dialogue with the public, thereby making it easier for both the students and the public to articulate what they meant (see fig. 5-6).

5-6. *Students with their completed model of the Mississippi River, which they took out to engage residents in their ideas for a transformed riverfront.*

"[I]f you're having fun, you don't think about the elevator speech you have memorized in your head," said Dorius. "It can be a conversation, it can be loose, it can kind of veer off a little bit, and that's okay. It's more about making the connections. You know, it's building the trust. So next time you can make more of an elevator pitch, but for now, be yourself, have a fun conversation."

After this experience, many of the students went on to be a part of a multi-agency/multi-player engagement team for another Mississippi River project called the Upper Harbor Terminal. Along with the Parks Foundation, the Park Board, a landscape architecture firm, the City of Minneapolis, and a local music venue, the students took the reins once again and engaged surrounding communities in their ideas for a reimagined space and how it might benefit a broad cross section of residents.

"They've been on this project for three and half years now," said Dorius, "doing a lot of [public] engagement, talking about bike safety, connections to the river, connections to downtown, jobs, affordable housing, bringing resources to North [Minneapolis] instead of basically bringing gentrification."

Students can be apprentices at Juxtaposition until they are twenty-two, after which "most of them have gone on to college, most of them are going into some sort of design field," said Dorius. "It's amazing. If they're not going into a design field, they're going into a field where they're really challenging the inequity of that field—that's their focus."

Chapter 6

Use Your Senses!

"With the first workshop, you are looking into the memory, and then with the pop-up model, you're getting people to play again and see and build together and generate ideas. Then the walking tour was experiential," recalls Ruth Gallardo of her experience with the engagement events in her extended family's hometown of South Colton and the tour's place within a larger whole.

Indeed, the walking tour is a logical progression from the previous engagement events. It's a way of opening up our senses to the world around us, to walk through spaces and places we may have traveled through hundreds of times, but this time to explore them with our senses amplified. Additionally, the tour allows participants to revisit locations they perhaps had talked about during the model-building workshop or pop-up model, but here they experience changes in temperature, light, shade and shadow, hard and soft surfaces, sounds of all kinds and volumes, among other factors.

With their senses awakened and attuned, participants are actually in an ideal position to be creative. As Wadehra said of the site exploration, participants get into a "sensing state, and into a sense of well-being and a meditative flow state," the combination of which creates the perfect scenario in which to be expansive with their thinking and to explore creative ideas. While these ideas will begin to readily flow forth throughout the site exploration, you may consider following the exercise with a model-building workshop. This is an approach we took when we worked with teachers at Rosewood Elementary Urban Planning and Design Magnet School in West Hollywood (see chapter 4). We had them explore the parking lot next to the school with their senses and then brought everyone inside for a team-based model-building exercise in which they then redesigned that parking lot into a completely transformed space (e.g., full of trees, water, green space, and hang-out spots, and with parking being only a small part of the transformed space). In the case of our sensory-based walking tour in South Colton, we chose to stick to just the tour but then provided the pop-up model at the end in case participants wanted to build any of the ideas they had talked about along the tour.

This tour is what we'll explore more in depth in this chapter. We'll look at where we were at this point in the project timeline, how we developed the route for the tour, what stories, memories, and ideas emerged along the way, and then how we folded everything into our increasingly fleshed-out ideas for a safer, more walkable, better connected South Colton.

Timeline and Sequencing

We planned the tour as the third in the sequence of engagement events, scheduling it for Saturday, January 19. Placing the tour toward the end of January meant that it was far enough away from the New Year and vacations, giving us enough time to plan and publicize the event while still allowing us to capitalize on the energy from the previous engagement events.

It is common for us to schedule the site explorations for the latter half of a project, after we've conducted at least one model-building workshop. This indeed was the case with our work with Rosewood School, as well as with bicyclists and pedestrians in Palo Alto for our project on making a shared bike/ped underpass under the Caltrain tracks (see chapter 2). The model-building workshops provide a forum not simply for dreaming but also establishing core values and aspirations; the site exploration allows participants to then see where both the possibilities and the gaps are in the physical realm for realizing those dreams and aspirations.

Tailoring the Tour to South Colton

Key to planning any sensory-based walking tour is a pre-walk to determine where to walk and where to stop and observe, and to ascertain how long the route will actually take. A one-hour walking tour is what we ultimately aim for, so timing the pre-walk is important. The goal is to plan a route that, on the pre-walk, takes about forty-five minutes to complete. In this way, we are accommodating for frequent, less-planned stops at the actual event, as participants will share ideas, thoughts, and memories that emerge as their senses and memory are activated along the tour.

In the case of South Colton, we knew we would not be able to walk the entire project area within one hour, so the challenge was to cover enough useful area and places that would offer up enough learning lessons for all participants—including ourselves. To help us focus and refine the walk, we drafted up a list of aspects of the neighborhood and project area we wanted to explore. These were informed by ideas that had come out of both the model-building workshop and the pop-up model event and out of the market analysis. They included:

- Problematic pedestrian crossing areas
- Examples of poor tree canopy and examples of healthy tree canopy
- A reimagined and revived Seventh Street

- The large vacant parcel at La Cadena and O Street
- Pedestrian connections between South and North Colton
- Examples of ways in which residents have enhanced both their yards and the adjacent public realm
- Opportunities for new nature trails and greenspace
- Lack of trees and safe street crossings around school

Our starting and ending point for the tour, Rayos de Luz Church on La Cadena, had already been fixed beforehand. This is where Dr. Luis Gonzalez holds his CityTalk community meetings on Saturdays, so it served as a natural gathering and starting place for the tour. Additional constraints included the fact that La Cadena, the spine of the project area and the neighborhood, does not allow for pedestrian crossing at every intersection (an urban design and transportation problem in itself), so we had to allow time for double-backs. The project area is also much longer than it is wide, so some areas toward the south were potentially too far out of the way for a one-hour tour.

In doing the mock walking tour, we wanted to not only solidify the route but also keep our eyes open to surprises and discoveries that we could potentially add to the tour. Indeed, this did end up being the case, as we added in a stop where we looked at how a resident had created sunken basins for his street trees so that they could capture rainwater and could water the trees more easily; we also discovered overflowing gardens that certain residents had made in which they had created a combination of both shade and space for growing fruit and vegetables (see fig. 6-1).

Out of the trial walk came a wish-list route of seventeen stops (see fig. 6-2). However, upon sharing the route with Gaurav Srivastava and the rest of the project team and discussing it, we ended up taking out some of the stops and modifying the route so that it covered a slightly smaller area. Specifically, we eliminated those stops at the southern end of the project area, as logistically they made the walk too long (see fig. 6-3).

6-1. An example of the overflowing front-yard gardens that can be found all throughout South Colton.

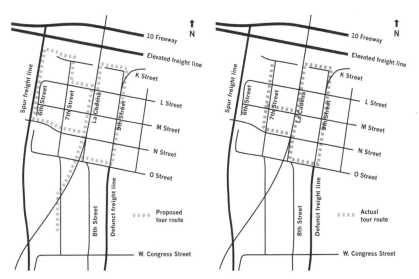

6-2 (left). The South Colton walking tour route as initially proposed.

6-3 (right). The revised South Colton walking tour route, which allowed us to get through the tour in about an hour while still covering enough useful territory.

Getting the Word Out

Key to publicizing the walking tour was piggybacking off Dr. Gonzalez's weekly, Saturday-morning CityTalk gatherings. These gatherings are very popular within the community and are already a part of many residents' weekly routine. Dr. Gonzalez had let his network and regular attendees of CityTalk know that immediately after the January 19 gathering would be a walking tour exploring South Colton's design, landscape, memories of place, and opportunities for change. As had been hoped, many of the residents who ultimately came on the walking tour were regular attendees of CityTalk.

We also publicized the event through our networks, and Srivastava of Dudek and Steve Weiss from the City of Colton did the same. While we did use social media as a way of connecting with these networks, we also made personal phone calls to those we knew in the area who we thought would be particularly interested in attending the event. As with our publicizing the other events, we favored making direct asks. Given that the social media environment has gotten intensely saturated, it's too easy to click "yes" to attending an event and then simply not show up.

On the day of the event, Weiss spoke at the CityTalk event itself about both the South Colton Livable Corridor project and the walking tour, encouraging folks to stay and join us on the tour afterwards. Many attendees had not gone to the model-building workshop or the pop-up, so they were unfamiliar with some of the project details, and so we were able to bring an even broader swath of people into the project.

Setting Out, Attuning Our Senses, and Exploring

At the outset of the tour, we made clear that while we would be leading folks along a planned route, the tour was as much an opportunity for the participants to talk about particular memories related to the places we visited and ideas they had as it was for us to offer our own observations and expertise. We also encouraged people to be paying attention to how the environment around them felt to their senses, and how those sensory perceptions changed as the environment changed. As this was the first time that many of the participants had been on an urban planning and design–themed tour, we explained all of this in a straightforward way: "Pay attention to what you see, how you feel, what you smell, whether a space is hot or cold, feels safe or unsafe, and what about the surroundings might be making you feel that way. If a spot brings up a particular memory for you, don't hesitate to let us know what that memory is." Our role as facilitators of these events is to engage everyone in the activity, so we try to avoid using any kind of jargon or "planner-ese." In any case, with that simple bit of advice regarding what to look out for, we set off on the walk.

Heading south on La Cadena, we quickly sank into a rhythm that set the tone for the entire tour: following the route but allowing for impromptu observations along the way. These unplanned observations would often spark other observations regarding something immediately adjacent to where we had stopped. Along La Cadena we came upon a sandwich-board advertisement on the sidewalk and awnings above storefronts. While not formally a stop along the route, we took this as an opportunity to talk about both elements and how they are unique to many Latino neighborhoods, and how they can both enliven the sidewalk and create a sense of shelter within it. At one point, we also found ourselves immediately next to red-striped zones on the curb, and a participant pointed out that the inability to park on the street is frustrating, given that La Cadena is a main street. We noted that the addition of parked cars could also create a further buffer between pedestrians and busy La Cadena, now designated a trucking route—hence the red-striped curbs. Further along, we came upon a mural outside of a convenience store, and James talked about how a simple intervention on the side of a building can completely transform the feel of a building's façade and the nearby street corner.

At this point, we were nearing the vacant lot at the intersection of O and La Cadena, adjacent to that is an existing small plaza which has seen better days. We stopped in the plaza and asked people about their impressions from a sensory perspective: not enough shade, too many hard surfaces, and everyone wished the fountain could work again. From there we turned to the vacant lot and talked about what people would like to see there: space for gatherings, music, restaurants, a market.

Looping around and north, we headed up to K Street, stopping along the way to stand beneath a dense canopy of carob trees and observe how we felt in the cool shade, and then looking at how a resident had planted his street trees to capture rainwater (see fig. 6-4). At K Street we wanted to explore one of the more unique aspects of the neighborhood: how residents have improvised within the parkways. Within this particular parkway, residents have created an ad hoc playground, a picnic area, and even an informal Italian-style arcade of arching wires and Christmas lights that loop over the sidewalk, along with several trees (see fig. 6-5). We asked participants about what effect these efforts had on the parkway space: more inviting, playful, shady, comfortable.

From K Street, we headed to the west side of La Cadena. Along the way were opportunities to explore what a reimagined connection between North and South Colton would look like and to see where new pedestrian crossings were needed to get across busy La Cadena. Once on the other side, we took the opportunity to hang out under the canopy of a massive jacaranda tree on L Street and observe how we felt underneath it as opposed to how we felt while walking along busy and shade-less La Cadena.

From there, we walked over to Seventh Street, once a commercial spine of the neighborhood before the freeway was built. The street contains a mix of land uses: a large church, vacant lots, housing, and light industrial and warehouse buildings. Many participants began recalling how Seventh had once been the "Broadway of South Colton," an observation that stood in stark contrast to the state of the street now. We took this opportunity to talk with

6-4. *John points out how a resident has planted his street trees in sunken basins so as to catch rainwater and make watering the trees easier.*

6-5. *A resident has adorned the sidewalk and parkway with a DIY arcade of arching wires and lights, Christmas decorations, and playground equipment.*

everyone about how Seventh Street might be revitalized. The ideas that people came up with included farmers' markets and night markets, street fairs, a tree-lined median, and a mix of new housing and live/work spaces for artists and artisans. Recalls Ruth Gallardo of that portion of the tour along Seventh and residents' memories, "To hear the history—like I didn't know that it had been busy at one time there. But you still see some remnants, and the possibilities."

Nearing the forty-five-minute mark in the tour, we headed South on Seventh toward the park between M and N Streets, with participants making observations along the way about trees and vacant lots and what had occupied the lots at one time. Upon our arrival at the park, people began to discuss what they saw as fundamental design problems with the park, problems that would perhaps not be perceptible to casual visitors of the neighborhood. They pointed out how a four-foot-high wall parallel to Seventh Street blocks visibility from the street into the park and that the space is primarily used for people who hang out and drink behind the wall. As a result, participants said they never felt safe in the park and thus never used it.

At this point, we were nearing one hour and made our way back to Rayos de Luz Church. As there was no pedestrian crosswalk at La Cadena and N Street, we had to do informal traffic calming by walking out into the street and temporarily blocking traffic so that the group could cross safely. Once at the church, we briefly set up the pop-up model from the previous engagement event so that folks had the opportunity to build any additional ideas onto the model and relay any final thoughts to us about the tour and neighborhood. The mood was upbeat, with people hanging around and recounting further memories of the neighborhood and simply conversing and taking their time before going their separate ways.

LEARNING FROM WANDERING

Not only were we able to gather further layers of information from the tour, but the participants were also able to see how their surroundings have influenced their lives. "Just seeing the neighbor-hood, on the ground, possibilities, and what it could be. You learn about the world around you and how it in a sense shaped you by how you had to get around—traffic, lights, people," recalls Gallardo of the strength and value of the tour.

Another tour participant, Jackie, reported: "What I noticed, a lot of people in South Colton still keep up their properties even though they were built in 1900. There's one man [whose house was built in] 1890, I think, I hope they don't demolish that because that's a historic little house, but I noticed that those people take pride in their little yards and everything, and [the neighborhood is] predominantly Mexican American." She also added that the tour was an opportunity to see both the comforts of the landscape but also what she saw as real gaps in that same landscape. "I enjoyed looking at the trees and bushes and everything that makes it com-fortable," she said—but it needs more trees, "especially on the streets—La Cadena [for example]. This town, I don't know what's wrong with it, but it seems like they're taking out all the trees."

And some didn't agree with every idea that emerged during the tour. Participant Adrian said of one idea to add more color to the buildings to make the neighborhood look less drab, "Bright build-ings and this and that. We have enough—I think we have enough of that already. We should follow the guidelines that the city has north of the freeway, containing buildings. North of the freeway, you can only paint buildings a certain color. South of the freeway, it's a completely different thing, and you're dividing the city. You're separating it now again."

Whatever the comment, we recorded the observations and the tour itself by way of extensive photos and notes that we took along the way, jotting down participants' memories and ideas. From there, we compiled everything into broad categories of information under the general heading of Points of Interest, which included the La Cadena underpass, the La Cadena commercial area, Seventh Street, the park at N and Seventh, mature trees and how residents were caring for them, and the vacant parcel at O and Ninth Streets. The specific findings around these we'll explore in the next chapter, which focuses on outcomes and how those outcomes were worked into the final proposed design overlay.

Where We Were in the Design/Recommendation Process

Prior to the walking tour, we had not wanted to do any serious work on designs, proposals, or plans. "We were still getting to hear from the community," recalls Srivastava. "One of the reasons why we wanted to hold off on more work was if we heard anything that conflicted with the really nuanced input we had gotten from the previous engagement events."

As the tour was the last engagement event before our presentation of preliminary designs and plans at the open house the following May, it served as a kind of turning point within the overall project. The period between February and that final open house thus became the team's prime working time for compiling all of the outcomes and ideas from the workshops, merging them with the findings of the site and market research, and coming up with a set of design and development proposals, guidelines, and potential zoning changes that residents would then weigh in on at the open house before we made any final changes and presented before the Colton City Council.

The next chapter explores all of those findings and outcomes in greater depth, looking at how we wove the findings into the draft proposals that we presented at the open house and challenging all of us to expand our very conception of what constitutes an outcome. Too often we think of outcomes of community engagement as needing to be tangible in the form of a plan, designs, a new park, a development. While these are indeed outcomes that emerge from the Place It! approach, a whole host of equally important intangible outcomes emerge as well—these include residents who have a better sense of their collective values; residents with a proactive and visionary approach to neighborhood change as opposed to a negative and reactive one; newly formed relationships that bridge different worlds and professions. In many ways, these intangible outcomes are what can give a planning or design project its real power as a community benefit, as they have ripple effects that can emanate out from the source, strengthening bonds and solidifying the social resiliency of a place.

Before moving on to this exploration of outcomes, we invite you to take a look at how the site exploration medium can be used on a more micro level to bring a group of seemingly disparate individuals together to explore both the public realm and a shared interest in an idea, what artist and architect Carol Mancke describes as a "community of inquiry."

Rethinking the American Front Yard

Objective: Creating community by way of an exploration of both space and an idea

Location: Machina Loci Space, Berkeley, California

Participants: The general public

Timeline: Part of a day-long workshop on rethinking the American front yard

"I was looking for some spot that could give me some sense of safety, but at the same time I really wanted to be in touch with my surroundings, not only to observe and be somehow part of it but also to have some privacy," recalls Kasia Krzykawska, professor of landscape art at Warsaw University of Life Sciences, on why she had chosen to crouch down and reside within what, upon first glance, had looked merely like a parkway overgrown with weeds. "And first, just on an intuitive level, I was attracted by a natural form—a sculptural form of the place because it had been shaped by grasses and weeds there. It was like a small valley,"

The participants of this particular exercise had just been set out upon a street in South Berkeley where artist and architect Carole

Mancke runs her gallery, Machina Loci Space, which was hosting a daylong exploration into the American front yard. After a presentation on the history of the front yard and then a model-building exercise in which participants built their favorite childhood memory of being in a front yard (or, absent a yard, in a space between the sidewalk and building), participants were asked to go out into the street and find a spot at the intersection of the public and private realms that they liked. They were to reside there for at least five minutes, letting their senses absorb what was going on around them and reflecting on why they had chosen that particular spot (see fig. 6-6).

6-6. Kasia Krzykawska, professor of landscape art at Warsaw University of Life Sciences, hanging out within a parkway of overgrown weeds and reflecting on what drew her to the spot.

On the surface, this seemed like a particularly challenging task, given that the street is not uniform or particularly picturesque but is instead what Mancke describes as "fragmented." "We have the side of a church, the side of a bakery, two empty plots, two abandoned houses, an empty lot with a gate across it," she explains. "And the fact that it's gentrifying and the fact that this particular block of street doesn't actually have any houses on it—it's kind of a weak link in the neighborhood idea."

Yet despite this sense of fragmentation, the twenty-some participants of the exercise were all easily able to find somewhere within the street that they liked and wanted to be for a while. Krzykawska had found beauty and safety within an overgrown parkway, another participant found comfort along a low-lying retaining wall between the sidewalk and the yard beyond. Others found the good along building faces and underneath tree canopies. Says Mancke of suddenly seeing all of these people exploring her street and attuning their senses to it, "I remember feeling that the activity made the street come alive." And recalls Krzykawska of looking around and observing the activity unfold, "It wasn't that huge, the space, and people were not that far away from each other, but you could really somehow feel the energy and identity of the small spots people had chosen."

One participant's spot in particular struck Mancke because it was so unexpected. "It was down at the end of the block where there's this funny kind of paved area next to the side of an apartment building," said Mancke, "but that paved area there, it's like, 'Why would you do that?' It's really unattractive, it's not for parking, but [this participant] was utterly entranced with the shadow play of the trees there and found it to be a very beautiful corner, and I realized she was right—it was beautiful."

To carry that activity into its next phase, and to bring that spirit of inquiry outside in, we had placed a large aerial map of the street on a wall within the gallery space. Once ready to come back in, each participant would mark their spot in chalk on the street or sidewalk and then come inside and find that spot on the map, marking onto it the location of their spot. It was a subtle exercise, but it challenged participants to shift from outdoor three-dimensional space to two-dimensional space on a wall indoors. And for Mancke, this part of the exercise was at the core of what she is interested in exploring through the events and exhibitions she holds at her space. "I'd like to bring the sidewalk into my space—you know, bring that public space in. In the same way that the café puts itself on the public land, I want the public land to come inside, and there was a little bit of a sense of that happening when people brought their proposals to that map," said Mancke.

From there, each participant or pair of participants (some had chosen spots in pairs) were given the opportunity to come up to the front of the room, point out on the map where their spot was, and then offer a short explanation as to why they had chosen the spot. "Some people had chosen places with mulch, others paved areas, others more natural," recalls Krzykawska, "but it struck me that we all had that ability to find a 'microplace,' each of us."

The next portion of the exercise is meant to be a team-based model-building exercise in which the participants will take what they have learned and experienced from the first half and carry that through to actually reimagine a front-yard space. While shelter-in-place and social-distancing restrictions have put this portion of the workshop on hold (during the coronavirus pandemic), Mancke makes clear that when the time comes, what matters is that the participants approach the model-building activity less through the lens of solving a specific problem and more through one of exploring an idea together. This collective exploration of an idea is what she sees as leading to the creation of what she calls "communities of inquiry," which form "over a series of events by gathering a group together and kind of generating ideas with them that then get taken to the next event. These communities are not necessarily around an issue. They might be, but they could be around a day out, an idea, a question—but the questions don't have to be anything like, 'What do we do with front yards?' They could be 'What's the power of that space?' or 'What's the possibility of that space?'"

This concept of the "community of inquiry" and the exploration of it have the power to bring people together to explore an idea through play while also challenging our assumptions about what "community" means. We typically tend to think of a community as more long-standing and formed around a shared ethnic, cultural, political, or religious identity, for example. But Mancke points out that exclusion is often part and parcel of the community's existence. "Any community is limited—it's limited by how it's formed—who's included and excluded," she says. But a community of inquiry has the power to eliminate some of that exclusion and allow folks to come together, however temporarily, to share in an exploration of something they all simply share an interest in. The site exploration as part of a larger daylong series of events exploring the front yard was one way of creating that kind of temporary community of inquiry where any and all were welcome and which resulted in every participant having a shared but slightly different experience of exploring a particular space.

For Mancke, those experiences can then be brought to the next event to add a new layer to it and to create a new community of inquiry, which could also include newcomers who had not participated in the first event. She is particularly interested in bringing in a reflection on the pandemic and how it shaped our perception of public space when we were all sheltering in place. "I think it would be really cool to take that up—if we come out of this [pandemic] and we say, 'Okay, what happened that we want to hang onto?' And here's one thing that we might want to hang onto"—that is, using public space in a completely different way than before.

Chapter 7

Outcomes: They're Not Just Buildings Anymore

"Hᴏᴡ ᴅᴏᴇꜱ ᴛʜɪꜱ ᴘʀᴏᴄᴇꜱꜱ actually lead to results?" is a question we often get at the end of presentations on the Place It! method. The question generally comes from a planner or architect, and the implicit meaning of "results" is "buildings," or, if not that, some kind of tangible infrastructure.

The truth is that Place It! approach can very readily and easily lead to actual buildings and infrastructure—and, in fact, it can lead to better-designed buildings and spaces that welcome a diverse range of users (case in point, the ultimate design of the 50th Street Light Rail Station in Phoenix and its emphasis on accessibility and comfort). Additionally, the Place It! method can lead to more-nuanced and layered plans and design overlays that are tailored to the unique characteristics and needs of a community.

However, we need to be careful not to place disproportionate value on tangible and physical results at the expense of equally valuable intangible results. These intangible results are a core strength of the Place It! methods of engagement and can have positive ripple effects across groups, communities, and neighborhoods well after a Place It! event has ended. Take relationship building. A simple model-building workshop and the sharing of childhood memories and exploring recurring themes can lead to a forging of new relationships that perhaps would not have occurred otherwise. Those relationships can then serve to lift each person up, strengthen neighborhoods, and, in turn, lead to unforeseen and positive tangible outcomes (a phenomenon we explore further in the online resources found on the *Dream Play Build* page on the Island Press website).

So this chapter is an exploration into not just the tangible results of our engagement in South Colton but also the intangible ones. We'll talk about how we recorded and measured the results—to the extent possible. Measuring outcomes of community engagement can be a challenge, especially when trying to measure the intangibles, so we'll both explore those challenges and talk about ideas for effective measurement. We'll also look at how we gave residents an interactive way to weigh in on the draft livable corridor plan that we ultimately generated from all of our findings and explorations of the neighborhood. At the core, we wanted to come up with a draft plan that truly reflected the unique cultural and physical character, history, and tradition of DIY urbanism in the neighborhood.

The Most Important Outcome

For those who are less familiar with the world of urban planning and design—and perhaps for those who have been working within these professions for too long—we will say that there is a tendency within these professions to want to demonstrate an acquired and somewhat rarefied technical knowledge and skill by way of drawings, designs, and plans that propose grand interventions of a spectacular nature within urban space. Chalk it up to ego and a justification of one's role, but also to a genuine excitement about design and urban space—it is an approach both common and sometimes not what a neighborhood or public space actually needs.

We had an inkling from Day 1, but then a firm belief after the walking tour of South Colton, that "radical and grand" would, in our case, be the precise opposite of a typical urban design plan: instead, we would be slight with whatever interventions we proposed. As Gaurav Srivastava said of how the approach solidified after the walking tour, "South Colton has patterns of public activity that any other plan, if done in a typical way, would just bulldoze over, and we knew that this plan should not and could not do that."

So while we would explore adding in new housing through a variety of new typologies, the creation of new gathering spaces, and how to breathe new commercial activity into the neighborhood, we would equally explore enhancing what residents were already doing to enliven the public realm—basketball hoops in streets (see fig. 7-1), mini-playgrounds in parkways, street trees planted in deep basins to catch rainwater, homemade benches under those trees.

7-1. A South Colton resident has installed a basketball hoop in a parkway, thereby transforming the street into an ad hoc basketball court and enlivening the space.

Inviting in the Intangibles

A focus on brick-and-mortar outcomes alone, and an insistence that they be met before community engagement work can be deemed a success, both casts doubt over what could be a very effective engagement process and risks skewing those processes to almost pre-engineer them to lead to concrete outcomes (which are not a given). Additionally, we know from our observations during workshops, pop-ups, and walking tours, through conversations with participants during and afterwards, and through interviewing those who've woven the Place It! methods into their own work (see the *Dream Play Build* book page on the Island Press website) that less tangible but equally important outcomes exist and result from these engagement events—outcomes that benefit not simply the participants but also the cities that may be leading the outreach in the first place. These less tangible outcomes include:

- Shifting from typical feedback heard at town-hall-style meetings of "more parking" and "less traffic" toward more visionary and forward-thinking ideas
- Increased community trust vis-à-vis municipal authorities
- Increased capacity to navigate the planning process and local governmental processes
- An increased sense of empowerment as citizens, designers, and planners
- Improved group cohesion
- More-positive outlooks regarding one's neighborhood
- An enhanced sense that one can shape his or her surroundings
- Relationship building
- And, perhaps most importantly, building bridges between seemingly opposing groups by way of collective play and an establishment of collective values (see fig. 7-2).

It behooves planners, design professionals, and even those whose everyday work involves community engagement to not simply

7-2. *Building bridges across communities: a police officer and local residents in Phoenix, Arizona, collaborate on building a model of their ideal community.*

acknowledge that these intangible outcomes are just as valuable (and sometimes more valuable) than the tangible ones but also craft engagement strategies and methods that allow for these intangibles to be brought to the fore.

How We Measure Outcomes—Both Tangible and Less Tangible

Measuring outcomes can be challenging, especially when we are trying to gauge both the tangibles and the intangibles. And yet to neglect measuring these intangibles seems to us a path toward conducting engagement merely for the sake of it without bothering to ascertain whether the methods have actually led to more meaningful and useful outcomes in the first place.

Our approach to measurement is to paint a picture of the cross section of outcomes that have emerged out of a project. In the case of South Colton, we did this by way of not simply collecting information about what participants built, said, and observed during the model-building workshop, pop-up, and walking tour, but also conducting exit interviews with the participants. What we wanted to gauge through the interview questions was whether the participants had experienced transformations in attitude toward themselves and their capacity to change their neighborhoods, and changes in attitude toward their neighborhood and physical surroundings, as well as any other intangibles that might not be easily discerned through the other methods of information gathering. We then looked at how all of these outcomes may have influenced the final design and zoning proposals.

As such, we have divided up our recap of outcomes for the South Colton project into three lenses through which to look at the events:

1. Tangible outcomes of the events, measured by way of the models and ideas participants came up with
2. Intangible outcomes, measured by excerpts from exit interviews we conducted with engagement participants
3. Specific ways that these outcomes were folded into the design and policy proposals

For the fourth and final engagement event, an open house where the proposed designs and policy proposals were presented for attendees to weigh in on, we will explore how we measured the attendees' responses and feedback regarding the proposals and how any of this influenced changes to the final design and policy proposals that were ultimately presented before the Colton City Council.

A. Community Model-Building Workshop

1. TANGIBLE OUTCOMES

To record these outcomes, we used two flip charts at the front of the room and wrote down summaries of each memory and model in large, easy-to-read print as the participants explained what they had built. We also wrote down the recurring themes the participants had come up with and documented the process through photos taken throughout the entire workshop. After the event, we took the sheets of memories and ideas back home and translated them into a simple write-up for the prime contractor, and posted the photos to a publicly accessible Flickr page. The results of the model building and themes that emerged are below:

Results from model-building exercise 1: Build your favorite childhood memory. (The complete list can be found on the *Dream Play Build* book page on the Island Press website.)

Larry: Grandparents' house with animals and fruit trees

Alma: Went to park with parents and siblings, saw roses

Phil: Playing with friends on O Street, playing kickball, hanging out with neighbors

Ruth: Walking home from school, stopping at a shop along the way, feeling safe

Bob: Swimming in the canals

Jackie: Going to the Colton Auction, where there were animals and cowboys

Vanessa: Walking to the library, getting a snack, and feeling safe

Richard: Playing kick-the-can with neighbors, and playing football in the streets; remembering all the businesses, and that there was a baseball field

Angel: Going to fiestas, walking along the riverbed, being a part of Cub Scouts

Madeline: Going to the Colton Auction

Randy: They used to close off the street and have a dance with loud music in the street

Dr. Sosa: Remembering when she suddenly realized she spoke English

Stacey: Moving out of her family home and feeling independent,

that it was a positive change

Distilling recurring themes is a subjective exercise; it is really up to the discretion of both the participants and the facilitators to give the themes titles that best represent the ideas that emerge from the workshops. We advise trying not to fret over categorizing each and every idea into a theme. Rather, allow the group to gravitate toward the themes they really see as the strongest within the lists of ideas from the models. The objective here is for participants to *feel* heard, not necessarily to see each and every specific idea represented in a final plan, design, or drawing. In our case, here are the strongest themes that both the participants and we ourselves pulled out of the models:

Walking; family; being outside; playing with friend—both sports and less-programmed activities; community events—either being at them or simply observing them; belonging; freedom; safety; church; school; history; longevity (i.e., multigenerational families); animals; ritual (e.g., always walking to the store to buy candy); language (see fig. 7-3).

7-3. *Pulling out the recurring themes from the residents' models at the model-building workshop in South Colton.*

Participant responses from the "Build your ideal South Colton" exercise include:

a. Arthur, Richard, Angel . . .

Make something like Olvera Street; revive fountain on La Cadena and O Street; buffer railroad rights-of-way with trees; Wilson School used to have plum trees, so they want trees back; clean and safe walking zones around school.

b. Antonio, Ernest, and others

A Colton that has less smog and dust and more vegetation; a landscape buffer by the train tracks; a community center with more outdoor amenities; around the church a plaza or paseo.

c. Linda, Ken, and others

More green space and more walkable, with improved lighting; a trail for biking and walking along the Santa Ana riverbed; daycare center; skate park; more restaurants, with parking.

d. Emily, Debbie, and others

Improved lighting and cleaner, with a safer, more walkable La Cadena underpass; more cafés and fewer liquor stores; a library in the lot by Wilson School; more trees; less wrought iron; more police and safety.

e. Ruth, Vanessa, and others

Beautified railroad areas; more walking paths (with surface materials that aren't concrete); more trees; more kid-friendly businesses; better and safer crossing options over/across La Cadena; less industrial; caboose brought down to South Colton; rehabbed historical houses and businesses; more trees.

f. Larry and Alma

More trees and beautification; small businesses; landmark designations; a map of attractions; school, church; better lighting in parks; sports complex.

g. Christine, Steve, and others

Ninth Street and a way to walk to Downtown Colton that is safe and tree-lined; fewer fences and side-yard fences; a beautified Wilson

School; fewer tire shops; bakery, market, gas station; more trees; a reactivated Old Ninth Street; beautify the empty field by Wilson; lower speed limits.

From this input, we distilled these recurring themes:
Trees and greenery; safety; cleanliness; small businesses that are not just tire shops; sidewalks, walkways, and better walkability; lighting; buffers along train tracks; safe routes to school and safer crossings; places for gathering.

2. INTANGIBLE OUTCOMES

For the exit interviews, we initially created a standard set of questions to ask participants of each engagement event. We felt this would lend some consistency to the information we were gathering. However, it became clear during the interviews that certain questions were too technical for some of the interviewees, and other questions did not feel relevant, based on the direction the interviews were going in. As such, in our run-through of outcomes from each engagement event (see below), we have chosen to pull out relevant highlights from each interview to help give a more focused sense of the changes in perspective that the participants experienced.

Additionally, we also realized in doing the interviews the inherent contradiction of doing spoken interviews in the first place: we were asking people to use words alone to articulate complex feelings, ideas, and perspectives on events that, at their core, sought to engage them through means other than just language. So for example, we observed in some of the interviews that the interviewees very quickly became quite negative about their surroundings and focused on current problems they were seeing as opposed to more visionary ideas they might have or came up with during the engagement events. While we initially found this to be discouraging, we realized that this dynamic served to further underscore the importance of using means other than just words to allow people to express themselves about their neighborhoods and cities.

So if measuring intangible outcomes is key to the project you are planning, engaging in, or following up on for funding future engagement work, we suggest another way of doing the interviews: conduct them in the form of a building exercise by way of prompts that could include (but are not limited to) "Build a memory of the walking tour," or "Build a memory of the model-building workshop." This way of engaging the interviewees with their hands will serve the same purpose that it does in the model-building workshops and pop-up events: it allows them to be more expansive in their thinking and to more easily articulate their ideas, some of which might be complex, less straightforward, and rooted as much in how they *feel* about a topic as what they *think* about that topic. Otherwise, if you choose to stick with the standard exit-interview format, consider organizing the responses around core topics or themes, as we have done here, and avoiding technical planning language in the interview questions. (Perhaps surprisingly, even mentioning the term *urban planning* can be confusing to some interviewees, who may not understand exactly what *urban planning* actually means.)

EXCERPTS FROM EXIT INTERVIEW WITH WORKSHOP PARTICIPANT ANTONIO

On initial expectations of what the model-building workshop would be like . . .

> "At first I was very nervous, because it was a meeting with the public, and as I mentioned, I did have some idea of how they function. One of our assignments in school was watching a planning commission meeting, which was very tight and, like, stiff when hearing the public talking to the commissioners and the commissioners answering questions from the public. So I thought it was going to be like that, that we would have this very dry, straightforward information."

On how the meeting differed from his expectations and why . . .

> "Instead of city officials just answering questions and being really bureaucratic, there was more involvement with the

people—more casual, friendlier, more inviting for them, where I'm pretty sure they felt more comfortable being there rather than at a very stiff community meeting.

"Once the meeting started, that's when we were talking about the project, and once we started breaking up into different groups, it became less intimidating . . . I mean just being able to split up into different groups and different groups being able to inter-act with each other—it helped a lot. Yeah, it was like a team-building project in general, and anybody and everybody who could help someone helped."

On how he felt while building his favorite childhood memory . . .
"I felt a lot like a child—in a good way. I felt very free, and very like, 'Okay, I'm using my imagination to make my own creative idea come to life with whatever tools I have.' And it felt very free because as, like, the tools that were presented—the different objects, it's your choice of what you get to use and what you want to have in your model, so I think it's very powerful when you give people almost like an unlimited amount of resources and tools to be able to use, you get a lot more out of it." (See more at the *Dream Play Build* book page on the Island Press website.)

———

EXCERPTS FROM EXIT INTERVIEW WITH JACKIE, A WORKSHOP PARTICIPANT

On being a longtime South Colton resident and her life there . . .
"Yeah, [I've lived in South Colton for] almost forty years. I grew up in Fontana, which is right next door. I moved back in 1969, I think, I bought this house. It's a historical house. The house is right in between La Cadena and Ninth Street. It belonged to the first—he's buried in the cemetery, he has a great big old monu-ment—he was a doctor, I believe. The house is 108 years old. It's all constructed of granite stone, which came from the quarry here, and the steel in the basement came from the Santa Fe rail-road—in San Bernardino there.

"I'm retired. I used to be an antiques dealer. I had my own business and I used to sell to these people who used antiques in the movies. My shop was in Fontana. I bought a lot of costumes when MGM closed up. I sold them to Heritage Auction two years ago, which sold all of those. Most of them."

On what it was like to work with her hands to build a memory . . .
"It took me back, back to when I was young. I'm eighty-one years old now. . . . It reminded me of a different time—where things were very important, what you had. It's not like today's world, where everything's plastic and falling apart. All these architects—these new-age architects—they're building stuff that will never stand. Compared to the historical buildings.

"I [built a model of] being at the auction in Colton. There was a very famous auction there on Valley Boulevard. My grandfather, who raised me, we used to go there for animals, ducks and pigs and everything, and I remember driving down Valley Boulevard and seeing all of these cowboys—you know, by, which is Valley Boulevard and La Cadena—I used to see them standing all in a row, and I used to think, *My God, this is a cowboy town.* That's how I used to think about it. And then from Mr. Hannah, who lives in the other historical house up the street, I got a book from him that showed all the downtown area, the way it was, you know the buildings and everything, and it's too bad the city fathers at that time took it upon themselves to tear everything down when they could have had a beautiful historical downtown.

"[Building my memory] took me back to a happy time."

3. HOW THE OUTCOMES WERE FOLDED INTO THE PROPOSED DESIGNS AND POLICIES

At this stage in the project, we wanted to hold off on drafting up any formal proposals or designs; however, the information we gleaned at the workshop set a tone for how we would proceed with further inquiry into the neighborhood and explorations into design proposals and policy changes. The strongest themes that we saw and that we sensed could ultimately be translated into design proposals, policies, and zone changes were:

I. The sense of loss of the neighborhood's once-vibrant commercial life

We explored options for bringing this life back into the neighborhood while considering some current-day realities, such as the fact that Seventh Street is now physically cut off from Colton proper, and the challenges of reversing years of disinvestment from the neighborhood.

II. Trees and greenery

We explored how existing trees and greenery could be protected while also creating opportunities for urban reforestation, taking cues from what residents were already doing on a DIY level to green up their properties and parkways and increase shade to protect themselves from the intense summer heat. We would also consider what species of trees could actually thrive in this environment on minimal water while still creating discernible shade canopies. Southern California municipalities have long insisted on planting climate-incompatible species such as southern magnolias (*Magnolia grandiflora*) and riparian-habitat western sycamores (*Platanus racemosa*), which are planted along La Cadena and are all dying or completely dead (see fig. 7-4). Neither species has fared well in the era of climate change, with less rainfall and more summer heat.

III. The sense of loss of a once-vibrant pedestrian life

We explored key areas for improving the walking experience within the neighborhood—which includes considerations not only of safety but also of visual interest and a public realm that is comfortable to walk in. Additionally, we explored the DIY ways in which residents were already contributing to a vibrant and comfortable

7-4. *Dead or dying water-intensive sycamores line La Cadena. Cities across the country need to radically rethink their tree selections and plant trees that are better adapted to the local climate, environment, and extreme weather events.*

public realm through their interventions along and within the public right of way.

IV. Public spaces for socializing and gathering

We looked at opportunities for renovating the existing gateway plaza to the south of the project area at La Cadena and O Streets while also exploring new opportunities for carving out public gathering spaces, such as in the large vacant parcel also at La Cadena and O Streets. We also looked at DIY ways in which residents have created informal gathering spaces within the public realm.

V. The unique character of the neighborhood

South Colton is at the confluence of several unique cultural and physical forces. It has a close-knit community of many longtime residents that spans multiple generations and is predominantly

Mexican and Mexican American. It is clear within the public realm that the residents have taken pride in trying to better their environment despite being cut off from the surrounding areas. Additionally, the neighborhood has a street layout that doesn't follow the typical grid of neighboring areas, and the vestiges of small commercial buildings interspersed within the residential area are still there, both of which give it the feel of a small town and not simply a neighborhood that is part of a larger city. The challenge we saw was to maintain and enhance these social and physical strengths and small-town character while trying to somehow stitch the neighborhood back in with Colton proper so that residents could feel proud of their neighborhood while not feeling like outcasts.

B. Pop-up Event

1. Tangible outcomes

For recording these outcomes, we provided participants with Post-it notes, which they could write their ideas onto and place next to their models. We would take a picture of them with their models and ideas and then place the Post-it notes on a flip chart behind the model. We documented the entire event through pictures and posted them to a publicly accessible Flickr page. With the Post-it notes and any additional notes written down on the flip chart, along with comments and ideas verbally conveyed to us, we were able to go back and write up a summary for the prime contractor. This write-up included:

We asked people the following to start the conversation:
    How would they improve South Colton?
    What did they like about South Colton?
    What problems is the neighborhood facing?
    Using the model, we asked them where they lived.

We divided up their ideas and models into two categories:

Challenges and Opportunities.

Challenges
  Safety was a big concern
  Traffic accidents on La Cadena
  Pedestrian safety: lack of streetlights
  Improve alleys for walking
  Streets not clean
  Homeless people in parks
  Illegal dumping in vacant lots; need cameras to stop dumping
  Improve recycling center, as there have been multiple fires there
  Remove strip clubs, as there have been problems there
  Bad air quality because of the cement factory

Opportunities
  Many people wanted to make the area a destination with more
    shops, restaurants, and improved nightlife—including the
    addition of a night market.
  Urban design
  Street trees: Add more street trees to improve air quality, aesthet-
    ics, and shade for walking. The trees can be evergreen or fruit
    trees. Start fruit-picking program.
  Façade improvements on La Cadena: Think about architectural
    standards. How to improve the appearances of the tire shops.
    Facade improvements could also include a signage and mural
    program.

  Additional miscellaneous ideas
  Create a rec center (planned but never built)
  A more welcoming environment for kids and families, for com-
    munity gatherings
  After-school computer lab
  Dog park
  Walking trail

Many lived in the area and expressed they had been there for many generations

2. Intangible outcomes

Excerpts from exit interview with Baltazar Barrios III, a pop-up participant

On the challenges of everyday residents expressing spatial ideas . . .
"Working at cities for at least two years now, I have seen how it's kind of hard for most average people [to read a map]. You show them a map of the city—or even when they come to me and they ask, 'Hey I want to do this [project],' they have a hard time kind of showing it. It's harder for them to engage with a piece of paper that's two-dimensional and it is maybe outdated and isn't reflective of the current situation. . . . For me you don't have to expect them to be an artist when they want to show something [they want to do on their property]. And we even encourage them to do the simplest plans like on an 8.5" × 11" [sheet of paper], but even with that, I still get people who are nervous or who are hesitant or feel that they can't dictate what they want. But with this [pop-up] model, it kind of throws everything out the window, all of those fears, all of that self-doubt."

On how people interacted with the pop-up model . . .
"I remember just the common theme of people coming up to the table, eyes wandering like 'What is this?' and you know when you explain to them what it's about, you kind of see that curiosity, that lightbulb kind of turn on. And you tell them, 'Do you want to partake in this?' And they get either kind of nervous or excited, and just seeing them [build what they want to build]. . . It was people from all walks of life: mothers with their children, seniors, even your average twenty- to thirty-year-old resident . . . people coming in for lunch, people coming in to buy something and then taking their time on the way out on a Saturday morning."

On some skepticism that planning departments will adopt the pop-up model as an engagement tool . . .

"I believe [resistance to new modes of engagement] is a mixture of being used to a traditional model and also not having the capacity to make that change. One of the things that I'm familiar with is, 'We don't have the money for it,' or 'We don't have the budget for it,' or 'We have to cut staff.' [But] there's money out there that can be shifted from different departments. . . . They don't see what planning does as something very important. You know, it's crucial to everyday life, and as times are changing, we need to make new models that are relevant to these new times and circumstances, but until more higher-level planners or commissioners or city council members open their eyes a little bit to allow for these kinds of creative solutions, I don't think that change is going to happen anytime soon.

"For my senior project, I interviewed a planning commissioner and staff members for the city, and I asked them the question, 'Would you want more people to be engaged with the city?' and they said, 'Yes.' So, as far as I know, they do want people to engage, but they aren't open to things that aren't their traditional model."

3. How the outcomes were folded into the proposed designs and policies of the final document

The neighborhood scale of the pop-up model allowed participants not only to see where they lived within the project area but also to observe and conceptualize the sheer lack of physical connections between South Colton and Colton proper. Because of this, we received even more confirmation that the final plan needed to somehow rethink and prioritize these connections. "Seeing the physical layout of the neighborhood, one could really then talk about it, where the connections are challenged," recalls Srivastava. "And that at the end of the day, at least from the City's perspective, this became a significant recommendation for [the City] to seek CEQA grant funding on how to improve the underpass on La Cadena and M Street."

The feedback from the pop-up model also reinforced what we had heard and learned at the model-building workshop: a safer, cleaner, more inviting pedestrian environment; more trees and greenery; plazas for gathering and socializing; more businesses that a range of people could patronize and walk to (e.g., cafés, restaurants, and bars as opposed to just tire shops and strip clubs).

C. Sensory-Based Walking Tour

1. TANGIBLE OUTCOMES

To document the tour, we used a combination of note-taking to record ideas that residents had at the set stops of the tour and other ideas that spontaneously sprang up along the way. We also made sure to heavily document the tour through photos—especially photos of portions of the tour where everyone stopped to observe a particular aspect or phenomenon of the neighborhood. For example, one stop involved standing under a very large jacaranda tree and then comparing how one felt on a sensory level underneath it to how one had just felt along busy and treeless La Cadena. The exercise generated considerable discussion and interest among the participants, so we photographed it from multiple vantage points to document how that stop evolved and the conversation and discovery it generated (see fig. 7-5). We could then use these photos later on to not only provide a visual record of what was said and done but also more easily convey what a sensory-based walking tour is when presenting the idea as a potential mode of engagement for a subsequent project.

Written documentation includes the following:

Point of Interest 1: La Cadena Underpass
Needs color, lighting, needs to be brightened up; plants and greenery should be added; people like the idea of having a new

7-5. Sample of the visual documentation of the tour. Here we were talking about how this mature jacaranda tree radically changed how the sidewalk felt (i.e., cool, comfortable, protected) as opposed to wide and treeless La Cadena nearby.

sidewalk that doesn't stay at grade with the street, but they were concerned that this might block the murals.

Point of Interest 2: La Cadena Commercial Area

People disliked that La Cadena is a trucking route and that the curbs are striped red in front of the neighborhood-serving businesses (there is no on-street parking as a result). The huge billboard at M and La Cadena could be a mural instead. There are very few trees along the street—many of the tree wells are full of trash and don't have trees in them. And they wanted to see the vacant parcel at O Street transformed into a large plaza and market area.

Point of Interest 3: Seventh Street

Walking up and down Seventh Street elicited strong emotions and memories among many of the participants—in part because the street's current forlorn state stood in stark contrast to participants' lived experiences of its storied past as the "Broadway of South Colton." Yet experiencing the street's almost complete lack of traffic, its mix of still-standing but vacant commercial buildings, vacant lots, and houses, served to spark participants' imaginations, and ideas flowed forth.

Folks thought that perhaps there could be a marketplace or flea market in the church parking lot when it's not being used. There should be a community garden that kids could access. A lane could be taken out on each side for wider parkways and a consistent line of trees. Benches and lighting could help. Ideas for pop-up events included food truck nights, a night market. Perhaps a planted median. Some said that many folks would walk to the event by way of some of the alleys but that the alleys need to be repaved and cleaned up, which brought up the Activating Alleyways project in Riverside.

Point of Interest 4: Park at N and Seventh (see fig. 7-6)

Take down the wall between the park and the adjacent parking lot to improve safety and security (almost everyone said that

7-6. Another sample of the visual documentation of the tour. Here we were hearing from residents about the problems they have observed with the park at N and Seventh Streets. We then discussed their ideas for a transformed and redesigned park.

the park is completely unused except by folks who drink there). There could be a farmers' market adjacent to it. The park needs to be more family-friendly with activities for people of all ages, such as lawn bowling, playground equipment. Needs better lighting. Apparently the sprinkler system in the other half of the park on the other side of the train tracks doesn't work properly and the sprinklers will run for an entire day.

Point of Interest 5: Mature trees and how residents were caring for them

The presence of several very large, shade-providing trees interspersed throughout the tour also became significant conversation starters, as the experience of standing underneath them stood in stark contrast to many parts along the walking tour that felt completely exposed to the elements, harsh and concrete-lined. Additionally, we looked at ways in which residents had planted trees in sunken basins in the parkway to catch rainwater and make watering by hand easier.

Point of Interest 6: Vacant Parcel

We were also able to walk to the large vacant parcel at O and Ninth Streets, where a spur line of the railroad had once been but is now completely vacant. They were supportive of adding in more housing and a new, walkable street where the train tracks once were. This feedback supported our initial ideas to lay in a new public street lined with townhouses through the site.

2. LESS TANGIBLE OUTCOMES

EXCERPTS FROM EXIT INTERVIEW WITH ADRIAN, A WALKING TOUR PARTICIPANT

On ambivalence regarding neighborhood character and how to enhance and/or preserve it . . .

"Bright buildings and this and that. We have enough—I think we have enough of that already. We should follow the guidelines that the city has north of the freeway, containing buildings. North of the freeway, you can only paint buildings a certain color. South of the freeway, it's a completely different thing, and

you're dividing the city. You're separating it now again."
Do you feel optimistic about the future of the neighborhood? How does this optimism compare with how you felt before you participated in the events?

"Somewhere in between. Like I said, there are no businesses coming in. People don't walk around like they used to. Everybody drives, even if it's just one block. Nobody walks. And when I told them—they were going to try to make a walking street down La Cadena, which is one of the main streets in Colton—I told them you're going to have to lower the speed limit. The speed limit is 45, and the majority of the cars that come from the south to catch the freeway, they're going 50 or 55, so nobody's going to stop unless you bring something interesting into the area, and I don't see that ever happening.

"People are coming so fast, at the underpass on M Street. There are signal lights at La Cadena and N. Man, oh man, I have almost gotten hit twice. In my vehicle. But I won't walk down there unless it's a parade and the police block it off."
For you to feel comfortable walking there?

"Oh yeah."
Do you feel like other residents feel the same way?

"Other residents? There's nobody walking around."
So in your lifetime you've really noticed a decline in people walking?

"Oh yeah."
When you were young growing up, what was it like? Were there just a lot of people walking around in the neighborhood?

"Oh yeah, people would walk around the neighborhood, go to the stores because they were open. There used to be one, two, three, four, four stores—five market stores in the area, and everyone would walk to them."
When did you notice it start to change?

"When they started closing down the stores. Families started closing them down. And that's been about thirty years, maybe even longer. Even we used to walk to our school, and it would take maybe ten minutes to get to school, walking, but nobody walks anymore. Where I live, because I have a grandson who goes to Wilson, we take him by car to school."

How many blocks is that?

"About six blocks. The [main thing] is we don't want him to walk by himself, and safety-wise, it's not the same as when people used to keep an eye on their kids. It's not the same anymore. We don't know who is in the neighborhood—there are too many people we don't know, who you don't trust, and they don't walk."

And so the less people walk the less other people walk?

"Yeah, same thing."

———

EXCERPTS FROM EXIT INTERVIEW WITH JACKIE, A WALKING TOUR PARTICIPANT

On what she noticed most along the tour . . .

"What I noticed, a lot of those people in South Colton still keep up their properties even though they were built in 1900. There's one man [whose house is from] 1890 I think. I hope they don't demolish that because that's a historic little house, but I noticed that those people take pride in their little yards and everything, and that's predominantly Mexican American, but it's just an area that doesn't get infiltrated with trashy builders and, you know, taking this and knocking this away and everything. I enjoyed looking at the trees and bushes and everything that makes— now this isn't our downtown—but everything that makes it comfortable."

So you noticed a lot of the trees but also noticed that the neighborhood needed more trees?

"Yes. And especially on the streets [like] La Cadena. This town, I don't know what's wrong with it, but it seems like they're taking out all the trees. They took my trees out in front of my house that were protected by the Historical Society. They were 120 years old, and they got some arborist—he's not even in the business anymore—to take the trees down, and I put trucks and everything in front of the property because I didn't want them taken down. That's one of the reasons why I bought this house, because of the trees. Well, then I come to find out—I asked the workers if I could have the stumps of the trees, and one of the workers said, 'You know, there was nothing wrong with these trees.' Maybe one. Well, they took six out, I think. It just tore me up, because you know the City didn't know what was going on here. That's how much miscommunication there was. They shaded the street, they cleaned the air from the freeway we breathe in—you know, they filtered the air—and not only that, everyone parked under them. It was sad to see them go.

"Would you believe now, the old roots of the old carob tree [they took out] are like a big giant bush. That tells me the workers were right—there was nothing wrong with the tree. They took out eight of our historical trees out.

"That's when too many people got their hands in the pot. I think South Colton needs more trees, more shade, and more lights, just make it homey again."

Did participating in the engagement events increase your sense of civic pride in South Colton? If so, in what ways?

"Oh yes. Well, you know what, I see more people around by me cleaning up their properties—adding, I'd have to say, trees. Yes. And some people have moved and others have come in because the property is still reasonable here—it's not like LA or anything—the majority of people take pride in their property here."

On neighborhood change . . .

"I'm a historical buff and I tell you I'm not one for making a complete change in a neighborhood, like pulling out trees and redoing the sidewalk into something else—I don't know if it's too late for this town. Just look at La Cadena, how they've changed everything."

On learning new things about the neighborhood on the tour . . .

"I found out where the old Wells Fargo building was. I had no idea. There were two historical buildings, one is on the dead-end street, where the church is [Seventh Street], and those buildings, they were 1870 or '75. And the freeway is in front of it there, unfortunately, but I didn't know that that had been the Wells Fargo building at one time."

HOW THE OUTCOMES WERE FOLDED INTO THE PROPOSED DESIGNS AND POLICIES OF THE FINAL DOCUMENT

The core outcomes of the walking tour and the interviews really revealed and underscored a collective feeling of a deep sense of loss within the neighborhood regarding its commercial and pedestrian vibrancy but also an eagerness to figure out ways to bring this vibrancy back. While some residents had differing opinions on more fine-grained design details such as building colors, the essence of the ideas generated and knowledge shared along the walking tour further solidified the direction the design and policy ideas had been moving in after the pop-up: an embracing of everyday ways in which residents were greening and enlivening their yards, sidewalks, parkways, and the streets themselves; a more comfortable and inviting pedestrian experience; trees and greenery; more housing; enhanced neighborhood-serving commercial activity; spaces and places for gathering; and pop-up events such as street festivals and farmers' markets. We presented these findings and observations to Srivastava and the project team, along with photo documentation of the event.

Ensuring a Visionary Engagement Process and Neighborhood Led to Visionary Outcomes

The time between the walking tour and the final open house, held on Thursday, May 9, at the Sombrero Banquet Hall, was devoted to translating our findings—both tangible and intangible—from the outreach events, the market analysis, and our site visits before and during the project into design and policy proposals, which residents could then weigh in on before we finalized them.

At this point, everyone on the project team knew that the neighborhood of South Colton was a unique case—a confluence of both years of disinvestment and years of residents, despite all odds, bettering their environment in their own creative ways—so we were all equally on board with taking a risk with the design proposals and recommendations: we would explore more formal and tangible design interventions such as the creation of plazas, mixed-use developments, live/work spaces, and adding in crosswalks; but we would give equal emphasis in the proposed plan to encouraging residents to enhance the public realm in their own creative, culturally informed, DIY ways.

In many ways, in the creation of designs, policy recommendations, and plans, we sought some kind of merging of formal and informal urban design—the formal being led by policy changes, the creation of new public spaces, architecture, development, investment; and the informal being led by the residents themselves, oftentimes in the form of what planners and code-enforcement officers would typically deem "encroachment": basketball hoops in the street, homemade benches and playground equipment in parkways, and arcade-like hoops placed over the sidewalk and adorned with Christmas lights, to name a few and all of which already exist within the neighborhood (see fig. 7-7). "These were all internal discussions at this point. We didn't know how the City would react," reflected Srivastava on what guided the design and policy recommendations the team worked on after the walking tour. "Ideally, we'd allow that encroachment, but it's very difficult to write that up in a policy document because it just flies in the face of how plans are done."

Indeed, there has long been a fundamental tension between formal and informal in conventional planning practice in the United States—and in cities the world over. Towns and cities want all residents to go through the formal process of getting plans approved or rejected, and yet residents and businesses are constantly making changes to their properties without that approval—sometimes

7-7. A parkway that local residents have transformed into a shady, comfortable space, complete with fruit and shade trees, benches, playground equipment, and assorted decorations. In many American cities, these resident-created improvisations in the public realm would be considered "encroachment" and thus disallowed by planning and municipal codes.

out of a shrewdness or stinginess, but sometimes because they are responding to a fundamental need, such as additional income by way of, say, converting a garage into an additional dwelling unit. Going through the formal channels would be cost-prohibitive for the owner, so they skip the planning process altogether. Of course, gauging whether an owner is responding to a need, or whether that owner is, say, a slumlord and a cheapskate is very difficult to legislate.

In our case, we knew that the kinds of informal modifications to the public realm that we found in South Colton were the result of a neighborhood pride and culture but also a lack of resources. So our intention was to lift that pride up by way of more formal changes to the landscape and infuse the neighborhood with more resources while still allowing for and encouraging the kind of everyday creativity and care residents had been putting into the neighborhood all along. Additionally, we saw this approach as simultaneously benefitting the core project objectives of creating a more enlivened and inviting pedestrian environment, as fundamentally the DIY interventions in the parkways and streets of South Colton are, at their core, a form of creating a more vibrant and inviting public realm. Adds Srivastava, "I [believe] practitioners like me and cities should be less deterministic and prescriptive about how cities evolve. Like there's a randomness to individual actions that makes places, and plans that place too much emphasis on standards and guidelines, at the end of the day, they inhibit that randomness, and you end up with sterile places."

All the same, our aspirations surrounding the public realm would have remained just that, aspirations, if we hadn't also acknowledged the realities of current zoning and market forces and how they drive modern-day planning and urban design. In our current state of affairs of being a public-poor / private-rich nation (which, to be clear, is not a natural evolution of affairs but rather the result of a particular set of public policies enacted over time), the market can end up playing a disproportionate role in how planning and design actually unfold. The creation of new, publicly funded open spaces, plazas, and parks is uncommon without private dollars footing part of the bill, and private developments tend to dominate what ends up ultimately shaping our public realm (e.g., while the sidewalk itself might not change, how a new development lines and interacts with the sidewalk will).

Thus the project work at this point had to explore how potential private development could benefit the public realm, and what constraints that might adversely affect the design of that development could be removed or loosened. Recalls Srivastava of this stage of the project:

I would have conversations and meetings with Lance, and lead him down a path that had him look at whether we could do live/work on Seventh Street, and that became an important part of our plan-change recommendations because we didn't want to introduce just pure retail on Seventh Street, because it would never just coexist with La Cadena. So what kind of development typologies and activity could be had on Seventh Street that invite visitors to the street, add some semblance of economic activity? So then live/work became an option for us, and [Lance] studied the feasibility of the live/work. He also tested the feasibility of the plaza [at La Cadena and O Streets] for retail, how much housing it should have, and then we also added a recommendation to introduce a new street along the old railroad right-of-way, Ninth Street, so he had to study the feasibility of that. The cost of acquiring the land, and the cost of developing and selling new townhomes along that corridor, whether they would pencil out—and what density that would require.

When it came to loosening or removing restrictions, we began to learn that many of our and the neighborhood's ideas, even if they could work financially, would not work given current zoning regulations. "One of the recommendations of our plan at the end of the day was to expand the downtown approach to mixed-use development to portions of La Cadena South and even Seventh Street," said Srivastava, "so at least there would be the policy framework in place to allow a new kind of building to develop in South Colton. For something to happen, you would need a developer who's willing to take a risk and come up with a compelling development idea that is sensitive to the community. The first place where that is likely to happen is the plaza area, because it's a large piece of land, it would have a significant presence, and one could market it in interesting ways."

Final Open House

To present what we had ultimately come up with, we held the final engagement event in the form of an open house on Thursday, May 9, 2018, at the Sombrero Banquet Hall, the same location as the first workshop. There were no speeches or presentations, and people could drop in whenever they liked between 4:00 and 7:00 p.m. Our approach was to set the core elements of the final plan up for display on foamcore and easels, favoring those components of the plan that were the most visual in nature (e.g., proposed building typologies, plazas, street sections, open spaces) and organizing any text around overarching themes (i.e., core values that emerged from the engagement events, and core themes guiding the design proposals). Participants could then rate the proposals based on a set of stickers, which they received at the sign-in table at the door. The stickers consisted of green smiley faces, yellow flat-affect faces, and red frowny faces. While perhaps at first glance seeming a bit childish, this medium served as an effective way of allowing participants—who ended up being a mix of those from past events and those who hadn't been to any at all (including students from the local junior high and high school)—to easily and quickly indicate their reactions to the proposals, and, equally, giving us a very clear picture by the end of the event what of the proposals the residents liked, what they disliked, and what they were relatively indifferent toward, as, over the course of the evening, the boards became populated with green, yellow, and red stickers. We also placed the pop-up model of Colton just outside the Banquet Hall in case participants wanted to offer up any new design ideas before the final document was sent to the planning department and city council for approval and as a colorful and visual entry into the event.

Some of the core ideas we presented for feedback are shown in the following figures:

7-8. *The vacant parcel at La Cadena and O as it looked in 2018.*

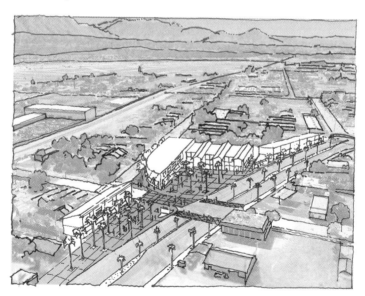

7-9. *Our proposed design intervention for the parcel at La Cadena and O. We presented this drawing at the final open house for resident feedback. (Drawing courtesy of the Southern California Association of Governments [SCAG] and created by Gaurav Srivastava and Dudek. Project funded through SCAG's Sustainability Program; project led by the City of Colton.)*

7-10. Our proposed design intervention for the vacant land at O and Ninth Streets, which included putting in a new street, sidewalks, street trees, and row houses. The design of the homes would allow for residents to easily interact with passers-by and neighbors and also improvise within their garden spaces. (Drawing courtesy of SCAG and created by Gaurav Srivastava and Dudek. Project funded through SCAG's Sustainability Program; project led by the City of Colton.)

7-11. The street section for the proposed new street at O and Ninth Streets. (Drawing courtesy of SCAG and created by John Kamp. Project funded through SCAG's Sustainability Program; project led by the City of Colton.)

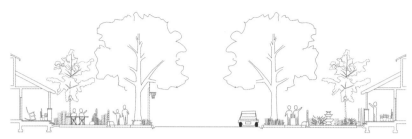

7-12. *Sample proposed residential street section, which encourages residents to green and enliven their yards and the public realm. (Drawing courtesy of SCAG and created by John Kamp. Project funded through SCAG's Sustainability Program; project led by the City of Colton.)*

7-13. *Proposed design ideas for Seventh Street. These included live/work spaces for local artists and artisans, and mixed-use multifamily housing. (Drawing courtesy of SCAG and created by Gaurav Srivastava and Dudek. Project funded through SCAG's Sustainability Program; project led by the City of Colton.)*

7-14. *Proposed street section for Seventh Street. (Drawing courtesy of SCAG and created by John Kamp. Project funded through SCAG's Sustainability Program; project led by the City of Colton.)*

7-15. *The existing underpass along La Cadena between South Colton and North Colton. This is the only physical connection between the two parts of town.*

7-16. *Our proposal for a transformed underpass between North and South Colton along La Cadena. (Drawing courtesy of SCAG and created by Gaurav Srivastava and Dudek. Project funded through SCAG's Sustainability Program; project led by the City of Colton.)*

7-17. *Proposed street-activation ideas for a revitalized Seventh Street. These included farmers' markets and street festivals. (Drawing courtesy of SCAG and created by Gaurav Srivastava and Dudek. Project funded through SCAG's Sustainability Program; project led by the City of Colton.)*

Typically at such an event, we would expect to receive extensive criticism of proposals, especially those that involved new housing and buildings other than single-family homes. However, any such widespread negative response was noticeably absent at the open house. By the end of the evening, the boards were populated by predominantly green stickers, a few yellow ones, and just a handful of red ones (and those all on the same proposal regarding affordable housing). "I was surprised by how positive [the response] was," said Srivastava, "because, at least from my perspective, there's always resistance to change, in any place, and especially because we had ideas for new residential [development] like live/work on Seventh Street, which is new stuff, so no one knew what it would look like, and then all of those townhomes on the extension of Ninth Street. When I was putting the boards together, I said, 'I won't be surprised if people push back on all of that.' But they didn't, and that was surprising. So we didn't take anything out."

In fact, rather than take anything out, we added in some new ideas that were offered up from the participants. The local students spoke to us about waiting for the school bus in the summer and how there is simply no shade, and how the heat from the sun can be excruciating. Thus we added in a proposed shelter for those students and proposed sheltered bus stops throughout the neighborhood. People also continually expressed that La Cadena is simply impossible to cross safely as a pedestrian, so we added in a recommendation of stop lights or signs, and crosswalks at every intersection of La Cadena within the project area.

When we asked Dr. Gonzalez why he thought residents were so positive at the open house and about the project in general, he said quite simply, "[The residents] have been ignored for so long. Their two biggest complaints are that there aren't any people in South Colton, and the City doesn't invest in our neighborhood, so they were grateful. You listened, and they really appreciated that."

One attendee to the open house said to us, "We just love this. We want change, we want restaurants, things we can walk to. We want investment in our neighborhood."

Ruth Gallardo saw the response as a surprise, in light of her own work on greening her Los Angeles neighborhood of Elysian Valley and improving both walkability and bikability. She has encountered extensive resistance on the grounds that such improvements will increase gentrification and displacement in the neighborhood. "It was so interesting: people [in South Colton] wanted investment— they were like, yes, bring that to us. They want change."

Indeed, there are real complexities in the modern era surrounding what happens when infrastructure is improved, a neighborhood is made more livable, and an increase in property values and rents can ensue. However, modes of community engagement that involve engaging residents with their hands and senses can bring memory of place, core values, and a range of creative ideas to the fore that otherwise would not have been there. Bringing these elements front and center and folding them into plans and designs in meaningful ways can lead to participants *feeling* heard as opposed to simply *being* heard. Whereas being heard is having one's two minutes at a townhall-style meeting and perhaps some nods and "hear hear's" from other audience members, really feeling heard, we believe, is being able to delve deep into one's own memories and experiences of place and build them; to participate in a process based on collaboration and sharing as opposed to transaction; and to see those ideas come to life and be validated in plans, designs, drawings. "The humility that this approach brings to the process, I think, is useful," said Srivastava, "as I think mostly people engage—planning and planners—they view themselves as experts, and the dynamic is that the experts are teaching the community, and I think the dynamic here was the reverse, and we wanted to stress that."

We don't have the silver bullet on gentrification and displacement; our market-driven system of accumulating wealth through property-value appreciation is something our engagement methods alone cannot solve; however, we do believe that our approach in South Colton of honoring and validating residents' own culturally informed, DIY ways of improving, enhancing, and adorning their yards and the public realm and making those informal interventions a core portion of the final design and policy document is a way of ensuring that a project isn't entirely market-driven. It is also a way of ensuring that the character of a neighborhood is as much a product of its residents' aspirations and personal interventions in the landscape as it is a result of more formal planning and market-based channels.

A Path toward Approval

Aside from the addition of proposals for sheltered bus stops, and crosswalks and stop lights along La Cadena, we did not ultimately change the plans and designs as presented at the open house. So from there, it was simply a question of presenting the plan to the city planning department and the Colton City Council. We were nervous that perhaps the parts of our final plan honoring the

DIY efforts of South Colton residents would raise some eyebrows and lead to requests for significant changes to the plan. However, in the end we received full support from the planning director, Mark Tomich, and the City Council ended up approving the plan unanimously.

If the approval of the plan had included the zoning changes recommended within it, the California Environmental Quality Act (CEQA) and an environmental impact statement (EIR) would have come into play, so these changes were not part of the first round of approvals. As such, the next steps will be for the city to explore and enact the zone changes per the recommendations of the plan and then do any of the necessary work surrounding CEQA findings and EIRs. As far as private-sector investment goes, "[the City] needs to find an enlightened and risk-taking developer to do something on that first physical parcel," said Srivastava. "But then . . . everything else will just continue as is, right? The neighborhood will continue to own and improve the public realm as they have been for generations. And now the plan says the city is flexible and will let them do that."

Learning from South Colton's Public Realm

The layered approach we took to breathing new life into the neighborhood of South Colton while embracing its unique character and culture was as much a product of the residents, their creative ideas, and their on-the-ground, time-tested ways of making a resilient neighborhood as it was our design and planning expertise. Had we simply gone in and done a Q-and-A, and perhaps a survey, we would have ended up with a project and plan that looked as if it could have been created for any neighborhood anywhere. Instead, we got something that was an unexpected mix of urban planning as we know it—designs, plans, drawings, zone changes—and an urban planning that, on the surface, seems novel but that is actually something we do all the time in ways big and small: adorn our parkways, add in a fence, plant a tree, put a basketball hoop in the street (even if just temporarily), hold a neighborhood gathering, craft ideas for a better tomorrow.

The irony in all of this is that much of the more informal, citizen-led urban planning that the final Livable Corridor Plan for South Colton was infused with and that we are firm advocates of is really filling a need that has been ignored: a public realm that enhances everyone's lives. The design and feel of streets, sidewalks, and parkways was long ago ceded to traffic engineers and their proclivities for traffic counts and reducing "friction" and making sure that motorists can turn right as fast as possible, among other perceived efficiencies necessary for a supposedly well-functioning city. Over time, this has led to a nation with a public realm that is, on the whole, unpleasant to be in and that leaves no room for doing anything other than moving through it as quickly as possible. The playground equipment that South Colton residents have placed in their parkways is a way of residents taking charge of the situation and saying, "Okay, if there is no usable park to walk to, and the main street through our neighborhood has been treated like a freeway, we'll do what we can to make our own parkways an extension of our yard and living environment."

As our nation further urbanizes, and more Americans are living in multifamily housing, something will need to give within the public realm. The street and the sidewalk are quickly becoming America's new front yard; however, absent some real interventions to make the street and the sidewalk pleasant to residents and not just convenient for motorists passing through, that front yard will be no place anyone wants to be in. It's our hope that urban planning as a profession can move toward having much more of a voice within the public realm and ensuring that every resident has access to shade, green space, places to walk to, space in which to interact and gather with friends and neighbors. In the meantime, it will be in places like South Colton that the public realm is pushed into the twenty-first century, as residents continue to creatively and resourcefully bring dreaming, playing, and building out into the sidewalk and the street beyond.

Where Do We Go from Here?

We chose to explore the South Colton project in this book for the countless layers of learning that it offered and still offers. As we've seen, the project was a merging of cultural exploration, urban design, hands-on and sensory-based engagement, market analysis, history, and looking at how to make a badly isolated space more connected and walkable once again. Because of these layers, the project has served as an ideal springboard for talking about the overlooked power that play and model-building can have in transforming neighborhoods in nuanced, positive, and forward-thinking ways. And that is a conversation we now have all the time with potential clients, cities, planners, architects, and community and advocacy organizations.

There is still skepticism, and there are still huge institutional barriers standing in the way of radically rethinking how community engagement is done. But there are also a growing number of people who are taking the Place It! methods out to their own workplaces and neighborhoods, oftentimes innovating off of and modifying the methods to meet the needs of the people they are working with. So what we want to do next, in closing, is to briefly explore what is hampering efforts to innovate in the realm of community engagement—but then we'll end on a high note by offering up suggestions for shifting both our perspective and thinking so that such innovation can be more possible, and you can put yourself squarely within it. Additionally, we offer up further avenues for discovery and exploration on the *Dream Play Build* book page on the Island Press website, where you can take a look at some of the ways in which people have gone through the Place It! workshops and then taken the methods and modified them to their own work and needs.

Conclusion

Play More, Talk Less

Iᴛ'ꜱ ʙᴇᴄᴏᴍᴇ ᴀʟᴍᴏꜱᴛ ᴀ ʜᴀʟʟᴍᴀʀᴋ of our tech-infused age to be privy to (or perhaps participate in) heated word-based exchanges whose participants believe their arguments will lead to some kind of clarity and closure. They never stop to question whether the medium itself might not simply always lead us to the same spot— more unwavering opinions, more reaffirming of existing beliefs, more polarization, and a closing down of the imagination.

This is what often happens when we confine ourselves within the standard lines of communication and never allow ourselves to sink into a state of play. And yet play is what we as a society need more than ever in order to shake us out of our rigid ways and our war of words, to establish shared values and open up our collective imaginations once again so we can actually envision paths forward—at the neighborhood level on up to our nation as a whole. "People sometimes think that civilisation consists in fine sensibilities and good conversation and all that," says Kenneth Clark in his 1969 program *Civilisation*. "These can be among the agreeable results of civilisation, but they are not what make a civilisation, and a society can have these amenities and yet be dead and rigid. So if one asks why the civilisation of Greece and Rome collapsed, the real answer is that it was exhausted."

Clark's words are all too relevant today: we are facing more complex and larger urban problems than ever before, and yet it sometimes feels as if we are stuck. We use mere language to engage around these problems, and the ideas that emerge are so often a retooling of what already exists: electric vehicles are our answer to global warming yet do nothing to solve our obesity problem, our lack of walkable streets, our pedestrian-fatality problem, our seas of asphalt parking lots, our building-in-the-urban/wild-interface problem, and so on.

But if we engage more in collective states of play, we can infuse our own selves and, by extension, a collective self with newfound energy and ideas. Imagine if, on a societal level, we could create that sense of vitality, energy, and lightness that Wadehra described. And imagine if everyone could be a part of that exploration and awakening. Our country would be all the better for it.

There Are Many Barriers, but Possibility Abounds When We Shift Our Thinking

Meager engagement budgets, a resistance to change, a perception that results generated from community engagement aren't useful, a lack of opportunity for doing engagement not tied to a specific project—all of these are real barriers to weaving more meaning-ful community engagement into planning and design processes (further elaboration on these barriers can be found on the *Dream Play Build* page on the Island Press website). However, community engagement, and urban planning in general, does not have to be conducted solely by way of formal municipal channels. Anyone can be a planner in their own way, and anyone can engage their community, family, and neighborhood in creative ways. What can slow us down is sticking to the common and understandable belief that urban change, community engagement, and the creation of enduring spaces and places can really only happen through formal planning channels. These are *an* avenue along which change can take place—and sometimes this is necessary, at least in part—but they are not the *only* avenue.

It is natural to think of planners as the sole change agents in the community-engagement equation. Not only is it their job to administer planning codes, craft community and general plans, and ostensibly guide how a city develops, but they are also frequently the only point of contact between the public and city government, one of the few municipal service providers that are required to engage with the public on projects of a particular size or scope. According to Alexi Wordell, a former city planner with the City of Oakland who has left the profession to pursue work in cultural studies at UC Davis, "I think in some ways, [planning meetings are] one of the few times [the public] feel they can vocalize something about something they are concerned about that could actually result in someone actually listening to them, and it's not a comment card. So [the planning meeting] can become a forum for just dissent, and for these larger issues that haven't been addressed but that aren't related to the project at hand." Yet planners rarely have the capacity to modify community engagement approaches in ways that would allow them to address these issues; they are tightly constrained by laws and protocol already set in place and are operating within bureaucracies that typically frown upon bold new ideas and innovation. In a nutshell, planners can end up bearing the brunt of an unrealistic number of urban problems that they simply do not have the power or the marching orders to solve. So, at the risk of sounding completely illogical, we need to step away from the notion that planners themselves are going to be the bearers of change within how urban planning and community engagement are done.

When we stop insisting that planners be the conduits for change within urban planning and community engagement, immense possibilities open up. Part of this shift also involves recognizing that "urban planning" actually happens on a variety of scales and within an endless array of settings well outside of the walls of city hall, and is something everyone can take part in. It includes everything from a resident of South Colton transforming their front yard into a verdant plaza to an interior designer such as Margaret Sullivan using a variation on the Place It! method to engage residents of all backgrounds in designing their dream neighborhood library. (Details of Sullivan's work, and two additional examples of Place It! ideas in action can be found on the *Dream Play Build* page on the Island Press website.)

"Urban planning" can equally include holding a model-building workshop with your neighbors to generate creative ideas for transforming the street into a space for play and interaction and not just cars, or lobbying your elected officials to put in more formal traffic-calming measures on the street—or perhaps a combination of the workshop and the lobbying.

When we recognize that we have innumerable options for participating in the shaping of spaces and places around us that don't involve urban planners per se, we can begin to be infinitely more expansive and creative with how we engage others in this process. Indeed, it is no accident that the Place It! methods were developed outside the walls of City Hall or a department of city planning. We weren't constrained by bureaucracy or timeworn protocol and could not only let our imaginations run wild but also respond to evolving needs within the planning and design projects we were working on. In this way, we could broaden out community engagement to include not just the traditional soliciting of feedback and input, but also a celebration of memory, of people, of lifting spirits and sparking people's imagination and creativity. More recently, during the pandemic we had to shift much of our work online and to video, to engage folks with their hands and senses but in ways that were safe for everyone. We also developed a method that involves participants exploring their neighborhoods on their own and documenting through video the places where favorite memories were made—a grandmother's front yard, a park bench, a restaurant booth. We then take these videos and splice them together to make, in essence, a virtual walking tour, which we all watch online and then segue into a virtual model-building workshop around participants' memories of place and their dreams for their neighborhood.

We as a nation have spent so long not innovating in the realm of community engagement that it feels as if there is endless room for creating ever more methods of hands-on and sensory-based engagement. As you think about what your role—whether you are a planner, designer, a resident who wants to better your neighborhood, an elected official, an artist, a dreamer—could be in engaging everyone in the kinds of enduring spaces and places we want to inhabit and spend time in, there are a few starting points we'd like to offer.

1. Start with clear objectives of what you want participants to both get out of the engagement and produce (e.g., models, photos, impressions, drawings, new attitudes, changes in attitude, an increased capacity to navigate the planning process). With the answers to these questions ironed out first, you can craft much more effective methods of engagement that don't fall into the trap of being all flair and no substance. There is too much community engagement nowadays that passes for being creative but ends up being gimmicky, whose results serve more as promotion for the facilitators' work than as tangible and intangible benefits to the participants and the community. To avoid this kind of situation, clearly identify the aimed-for tangible and intangible outcomes first. Yes, promotion of one's work is important and necessary for reaching a broader audience, doing more work, and making a living (yes, we have to promote our work, too), but don't let that be the sole driving force of the engagement.

2. In crafting your media of engagement, favor the hands and

the senses as the foundational media of engagement. As we have seen throughout this book, relying on language alone will invariably constrain participants and limit the scope and creativity of their ideas; engaging them with their hands and senses will do the opposite. It is not as if you must all-out avoid using words and language within the engagement, but don't let this be the primary or sole medium of engagement.

3. Start small. Those of us interested in creating change are, by our nature, keenly aware of the scope of the problems and challenges facing our world; however, don't let this scope of the problem or problems drive your initial attempts at engagement. You'll invariably get discouraged, burn out quickly, and also skip a little necessary tweaking and prototyping along the way to get to a set of engagement methods that are truly effective. Try out your engagement approaches with a small group of friends, family, and/or neighbors. (Yes, we've done this; we've had our families build their favorite childhood memories as a cocktail-hour activity; everyone learned things—positive things!—about each other that they hadn't known before.) Document the process for your own learning and be sure to ask for participants' feedback on their experiences of going through the process. Use both sets of information as a way of refining and modifying your approach(es) to ideally maximize what the participants get out of the process and generate the kinds of information useful to creating the kinds of enduring spaces and places that are tailored to your community, town, neighborhood.

4. Ask yourself how the participants will be empowered by the process; weave your answers into your overall strategy and approach. Shifting our approaches to engagement away from mere information-sharing to knowledge production means ensuring that it is not just the facilitators who emerge from the process with new knowledge and power. Everyone should leave the process better equipped to be their own planners, designers, community-engagers, change agents.

5. Infuse all of your efforts with joy, curiosity, and playfulness—in whatever forms those might take. While we don't want to force anyone to have fun, it bears reminding that in the face of sometimes dire problems, we can forget that joy, curiosity, and playfulness are not only what will keep us going throughout our efforts but also what will invariably make our engagement appealing to a larger audience and generate the kinds of creative and visionary ideas necessary to tackle those very problems in the first place.

All of this being said, the driver of this work should not simply be to solve problems on merely a policy level. There is a frustrating tendency among many change agents to regard considerations of design and the physical world as a kind of frosting or fluff that isn't necessary for solving "real" problems. However, we can't forget that the physical world has a direct bearing on how we feel, our well-being, opportunities for exploration, discovery—on our lives and how we live them. Grounding efforts for change within the physical and natural world of three-dimensional space can not only give form and tangible substance to change efforts but also lead to the kinds of enduring spaces and places that we all need in our lives every day. With more people living in smaller spaces, with more people seeking solace in nature and the out-of-doors, with newly heightened considerations of public health and how people can safely gather, the look, feel, and shape of the public realm and our outdoor world matter more than ever.

"Adios, Amigos" says the sign within the forlorn plaza along La Cadena heading south out of South Colton. But what else could it say, and what else could this plaza be? As the residents of South Colton made clear in the models and memories they built, the plaza doesn't have to be forlorn, the fountain doesn't have to run dry, and the whole space doesn't have to be devoid of shade and greenery. They imagine and envision so much more.

What spaces and places within your community deserve a similar rethink? In what ways would you mine people's core values and

C-1. Signage indicating that you are now leaving the neighborhood of South Colton. Thanks for stopping by, and thanks for reading.

engage everyone in re-envisioning these spaces? How would you translate those ideas, values, and visions into a better reality? Our hope is that now you will have a much better idea of how to answer some, if not all, of these questions, and blaze a trail forward.

Acknowledgments

There are lots of people within our orbit who have been instrumental in making both this book and our work possible: both of our respective families; people we interviewed for the book; those who gave generously to our crowdfunding efforts; people who've participated in our workshops, believed in us, hired us; and our editors and publisher, Island Press, for believing in this project.

We'd like to make mention of them here:

The Kamp Clan: Nell, John, Keon, Diana, Kendall, Genie, Kate, Kerry.

The Rojas Clan: Grandma Flora, Teresa Lucky, and Laura, Gary, and Dennis.

Those we interviewed: Roché Wadehra, Alexi Wordell, Ali Celebron-Brown, Adrian Chavez, Antonio Lopez, Baltazar Barrios III, Carol Mancke, Coal Dorius, Councilmember Dr. Gonzalez, Gaurav Srivastava, David Carey, Kasia Krzykawska, Jackie Ficarotta, Rebecca Karp, Grant Meacci, Patti Munoz, Robin Abad-Ocubillo,

Rosie Mesterhazy, Ruth Gallardo, Gerardo Sandoval, Margaret Sullivan, and Yetunde Zannou.

Those who helped fund the project: David Sundell, Lupe Vela, Diana Kamp, Mara Mintzer, Clara Irazabal, Jeff Hou, John Yi, Sojin Kim, John Shapiro, Annie Koh, Jim and Sue Gilbert, Samuel Bloch, Sandra Kulli, Jordan Jackson, Christopher Barnett, Shalini Agrawal, Vinit Mukhija, Marc Caswell, Norma Lopez, Martha Ramirez, Roberto Bedoya, Ian McCain, Pablo811, Greg Laynor, Dennis Rojas, Beth Martin, Jennifer Ly, Sarah White, Jesus Baragas, Sarah Wilkes, Jennifer Rangel, Genie Smith and Kate Tyler, Doug Blandy, Paul Lee, Leah Nichols, Marco Iniguez, Jonathan Pacheco Bell, Joanna Smith, Charlie Simpson, Marina Brown, Nell Kamp, Hannah Day-Kapell, Deana Mitchell, Peter Peterson, Jen Mein, Darcy Kitching, Anna Maria Larson, Carol Mancke, Murdoch Martin, Jeanne Schulze, Bethany Bingham, NewStreet2000, Nathan Keibler, Buckley Yung, Fay Darmawi, Andrea Garfinkel-Castro, David Freudenthal, Elva Yanez, John Muñoz, Larry Vale, and Elizabeth Farry.

Members of LA's art world: Adrian Rivas, Armondo Duron, Drew Oberjuerge, Leslie Ito, Ichiro Irie, Carmen Argote, Anne Bray, Sara Daleiden, Karen Mack, Terry Scott, Ben Caldwell, Chelo Montoya, and other artists and curators who allowed us to experiment through their world.

Minneapolis folks: Roger and DeAnna Cummings, Kristen Murray, Jen Mein, and Liz Zilka.

Los Angeles peeps: John Shapiro, Eve Baron, Cynthia Nikitin, Dorothy Le Suchkova, Beth Bingham, Jeanena Dupont, Adonia Lugo, and Joanna Bernstein.

Phoenix peeps: Kathleen M. Bartolomei and Greg Esser.

Past educators and thinkers who've shaped our thinking and writing: Mim Kagol, Meryll Page, Jonathan Cutler, Sandra Wong, Vinit Mukhija, John Chase, and Jane Blumenfeld.

Those who helped brainstorm ideas for the book title: Nina Rubin, Carol Mancke, Richard Spencer, and Kasia Krzykawska.

Special thanks to Gilda Hass for creating the City of Play video, Al Zelinka for giving this movement a name, and to Jennifer Allen for training us in the ways of effective crowdfunding.

And many thanks to our editors, Courtney Lix and Elizabeth Farry, for guiding us through the process and helping us hone the manuscript down into something that is—we hope—an illuminating and good read.

Notes

Preface

1. Steve Cimino, "Being Creative Is Complicated," *Architect* (February 7, 2018), https://www.architectmagazine.com/aia-architect/aiavoices /being-creative-is-complicated_o.

Chapter 1

1. Raj Chetty et al., "Where Is the Land of Opportunity? The Geography of Intergenerational Mobility in the United States," *Scholars at Harvard* (website), June 2014, https://scholar.harvard.edu/files/hendren/files /mobility_geo.pdf.

2. Katherine Levine Einstein, Maxwell Palmer, and David Glick, "Who Participates in Local Government? Evidence from Meeting Minutes," *Perspectives on Politics*, June 29, 2018, https://www.dropbox.com/s /k4kzph3ynal3xai/ZoningParticipation_Perspectives_Final.pdf?dl=0.

3. Wadehra says this about creating a space for play: "You're entering a liminal zone, which is essentially a zone which is neither this nor that, but it has its own special reality. You enter a football field, you enter any game, whenever you play something, you're entering a space with a certain set of rules, a certain set of ways of being, and then there is this whole ritual of entering, and there's a ritual of exiting."

4. When we use our hands, we "allow ourselves to drop into a completely different experience and use our senses to connect to our limbic brain,

[which is] loosely the seat of emotions, directly accessed by the senses, and where nonverbal ways of accessing [the world] actually work," says Wadehra.

5. "When you are engaging in a state of play, which is what the imagination helps us do," says Wadehra, "you are creating possibilities within the mind and the brain of more synapses firing, so more of the brain is getting lit up. And that gives us a sense of vitality, of energy, of lightness. We're on this kind of high alert but not a negative high alert. It's kind of like a sense of excitement and possibility that's happening. And that state of play is . . . a very altered state of being in some ways. It's a state of loose connections where older grooves and rigid ways of being that have gotten patterned into our synapses are getting loosened up a bit, so we're no longer responding from that regular, rigid way of what we already know, but we are open to exploration and possibility."

Chapter 2

1. Note that for groups larger than twenty-five, it can become too time-consuming to have each and every participant report back. In these cases, it can work better to have each participant report to those at their table, and then one representative from each table can give one or two highlights from each table to the larger group.

Chapter 3

1. "In the Sunshine of Neglect: Defining Photographs and Radical Experiments in Inland Southern California, 1950 to the Present," *UCR Arts* (website), University of California, Riverside, January 19, 2019, https://ucrarts.ucr.edu/Exhibition/in-the-sunshine-of-neglect.
2. Dr. Tom Rivera, professor emeritus at California State University, San Bernardino, recounts that Ralph Cervantes, a Mexican American, sued the City of Colton for not allowing him to buy a house in North Colton. Cervantes won his case, and gradually North Colton became more integrated. See: Dr. Tom Rivera, "The South Colton Oral History Project," *California Humanities* (website), September 21, 2016, https://calhum.org/the-south-colton-oral-history-project/.
3. Ibid.

Chapter 4

1. By *parkway* we refer to the planting strip located between the sidewalk and the street. The name for this space varies from region to region. In

Texas, it's called a hellstrip, and in Minnesota it's called a boulevard. In California, it is referred to as a parkway. As the project took place in California, we will refer to the space as such.

2. In this case, chicanes are steel dividers that narrow the entry points for both bikes and peds with the intention of slowing the bicyclists down.

Chapter 5

1. That is, existing height, density, and use limits constrain what can be built to the point that it would not be economically feasible to build on any of the available parcels within the neighborhood.

About the Authors

James Rojas is an urban planner, community activist, educator, and artist who runs the planning, model-building, and community-outreach practice Place It!. He is an international expert in public engagement and has traveled around the United States, Mexico, Canada, Europe, and South America, facilitating over 500 workshops, and building more than 100 interactive models. His research has appeared in the *New York Times*, the *Los Angeles Times*, *Dwell*, and *Places*, as well as numerous books.

John Kamp runs the landscape, urban design, and engagement practice Prairieform. He has developed innovative tools to engage people of all ages and backgrounds in both design and the natural world, with two decades of experience leading hands-on interactive workshops with James Rojas of Place It!. He frequently translates the findings and outcomes of those workshops into designs for inclusive and livable streets and neighborhoods that leave room for all residents to improvise and help create a more welcoming public realm.